UNICORN MAGIC

How to Manifest Your Desires by Living a
Life of Divine Love

Kitty Bishop, Ph.D.

BALBOA.
PRESS

Balboa Press books may be ordered through booksellers or by contacting:

Balboa Press
A Division of Hay House
1663 Liberty Drive
Bloomington, IN 47403
www.balboapresspress.com
1-(877) 407-4847

Because of the dynamic nature of the Internet, any Web addresses or links contained in this book may have changed since publication and may no longer be valid. The views expressed in this work are solely those of the author and do not necessarily reflect the views of the publisher, and the publisher hereby disclaims any responsibility for them.

ISBN: 978-1-4525-0000-3 (sc)
ISBN: 978-1-4525-0001-0 (e)

Library of Congress Control Number: 2010911325

Printed in the United States of America

Balboa Press rev. date: 7/29/2010

Dedication

I dedicate this work to my two beautiful sons, Kiran and Elias, who continue to inspire, teach and challenge me every day.

Note to the Reader

Throughout this book, communications from a higher source, the psychic children and the angels and unicorns are set in double quotation marks, while Kitty's own questions, thoughts and impressions are rendered in italics.

Contents

CHAPTER 1

A Quest for Truth: Who are the Unicorns?

Now I will believe that there are unicorns...
- William Shakespeare (The Tempest)

The Call of the Unicorns

In October 2009, I travelled from my house in Evershot in southwest England to London to attend Doreen Virtue's "Miracles of Archangel Michael" seminar together with my friend Carrie Richards. We had a fantastic time, meditating and sharing inspiring experiences, insights and stories. During the lunch break, Carrie started telling me about another spiritual workshop she had recently attended and which she described as "one of the best days of my life". Of course I was curious to know more. Carrie explained that she had been attending a course on Unicorns and had been attuned to the Unicorn Energy Healing System by Flavia Kate Peters, an Angel Therapy Practitioner who had been trained by Doreen Virtue in Hawaii. Since childhood, I have had a great love for unicorns. They stir something up inside me, and as a young girl, I had been an avid reader of unicorn stories. I often dreamed of them as really existing and could almost feel the reality of their beautiful, illuminating presence; their innocence, purity and unconditional love. As Carrie spoke about the "Unicorn Day" she had experienced, her face lit up as it reflected the excitement, joy and inspiration of that day in her memory. My reaction surprised me. I felt a deep soul urge to connect with the unicorns in this way and learn about how to tune into their healing energy. From the moment I heard Carrie's story of spending a day in the company of the unicorns, learning all about these wonderful creatures and how to harness their healing energy for the good of others and the planet, I had a single-minded desire to attend one of these workshops myself.

As soon as I returned home to Dorset from the Angel Workshop in London I started researching "unicorn courses" on the Internet. At the time, we were living rurally, in a picturesque little village which Thomas Hardy used as a setting for his novels, so it was always difficult to find any local events in the mind, body, spirit field. This time though I discovered that no matter how far I was willing to travel, there were no unicorn workshops available at all. It seemed that this was a very new form of healing energy, and there were not many people, and even fewer teachers, who had come into contact with it yet.

I was very disappointed. I felt wholly determined to get in touch with the unicorn energy. I had a deep sense of knowing that this was what I was meant to do. As a next step, I started researching books and information on unicorns, but it seemed that most publications just gave the conventional history of the unicorn as a "fabled beast" that was a popular character in fairy tales, myths and legends. That was not the sort of information I was interested in. I was searching for metaphysical explanations of the unicorn energy, what it signified in relation to healing and the evolvement of consciousness, its deeper mystical meaning, and why the unicorns were choosing this day and age to come back to Earth and connect with people on this planet. As I was getting nowhere with my inquiries, I decided to turn off my computer and get ready for bed.

Because I have two young sons, the time at night before I go to sleep is really the only time I have purely to myself. I always use it to indulge in my passion for spiritual books (I am an avid reader and have an inexhaustible library!) and to meditate. My daily meditation practice is very important to me. I am what you could call a "practical mystic", someone who seeks guidance from the ultimate power and intelligence of the universe to improve everyday life. Meditation for me is the key to contacting and maintaining contact with ultimate intelligence.

My Unicorn Attunement

As I was sitting in meditation that night, I felt myself slipping into a very deep state of consciousness. All of a sudden, my body seemed to completely dissolve and I was as big as the universe. I felt an immense outpouring of unconditional love. My heart chakra was filled with a very bright, pure golden light that kept growing until it felt as though there was nothing else, just this pure, luminous golden light and a feeling of boundless, unconditional love. As I felt the waves of love and light pulsating through me, I suddenly noticed a strong pressure on my forehead, just between my brows in the location of the third eye. As I concentrated my attention on this area, I had a vision of a spiralling, vortex-like golden energy shooting upwards from my third eye in the shape of a cone; magnificent, glittering and sparkling. It looked exactly like a unicorn horn, not physical, but an ethereal energy-consciousness vision of it. I was viewing the world through this "eye", this unicorn horn energy vortex. I saw everything in brilliant colours, bathed in light and infused by love. I had a thought: *This is how Source must view everything. I am seeing through the eyes of Source.* As I sat in complete wonder and amazement at what was happening, I suddenly heard a voice say, "This is your unicorn attunement". I knew instantly that this was true. I felt a huge wave of gratitude as I realized that my single-minded desire to connect with the unicorns and understand their energy nature, had brought me into alignment with their frequencies and called forth this beautiful experience of self-attunement. I felt incredibly blessed and thankful and went to sleep blissfully happy. My dreams were filled with unicorns, of course!

The next day I sat down and very excitedly typed out an email to Carrie, relating my experience in meditation and my theory that unicorns were an "archetype" of unconditional love and the awakened third eye. Christ said, "If thine eye be single, thy body shall be filled with light". (Matthew 6:22) The "single eye" Christ was referring to is the mystical Third Eye, or the Eye of the Soul. In meditation, we have our physical eyes closed, with the result that the "inner eye" opens up and the mind begins to see into itself.

At this point I had only my own experience to go on as I had not been able to find a metaphysical explanation of unicorns and their frequencies or energy nature anywhere. Carrie wrote back saying that my meditation experience exactly mirrored what she had learned in her course. She felt that the attunement I had been given in meditation signalled that I had a strong connection with the unicorns. They wanted to work with me, no doubt about it. There was more unicorn magic to come. I have found that when the unicorns find someone that they feel will make a suitable conduit for their energy, helping them spread their message of Divine love on this planet, they will make their wishes heard loud and clear. They are also very good at lining up synchronistic events, sending signs, and arranging events which make it impossible to ignore that "you have been called".

A Day with the Unicorns

One such event was lining up for me now. Carrie wrote to me saying that Flavia Kate was offering another unicorn workshop in two months time. It was to be only the second one she had ever given. Naturally, I jumped at the chance. Now that I had personally experienced the incredibly powerful and beautiful energy of the unicorns, I felt even more strongly than before that this was something I simply had to do, no matter how far I had to travel or how difficult it would be to arrange childcare, time off work, and all the other mundane, but important, aspects of my life. During the Archangel Michael workshop in London, Doreen mentioned something that resonated with me. She told the audience that she always prays before her workshops that everyone who is called to attend will have sufficient funds, childcare provisions, time off work, travel arrangements, and so on, to be able to participate. This is exactly how I felt about this Unicorn Workshop offered by Flavia Kate. I simply had to be there and I knew that the details would be taken care of for me by a Higher Power. And that's exactly what happened.

The workshop took place in The Well-Being Centre in Newbury, Berkshire. Immediately upon entering the building I could sense a very clear, calm and uplifting energy. It was truly a sanctuary in the midst of the noise, activity and hustle-bustle of everyday suburban life outside. It even had a fairy garden with a wishing well filled with crystals in the back. I instantly knew that this would be a magical day. As we sat in a semi-circle and introduced ourselves, I soon discovered that all of us were there because we had felt a strong pull, push, or nudge to attend. When the turn came to introduce myself, I talked about my meditation experience in which I had received an attunement into the unicorn energy directly from my Higher Self (or directly from the unicorns?). I knew intuitively that unicorns are illuminated creatures which are members of the angelic hierarchy. Unicorns are an aspect of Divine Mind expressing Itself as Divine Love. In my third eye, I saw their horns as emanations of pure light, which has the power to enlighten, inspire and heal. Unicorn horns are like magic wands that pour out Divine energy. Wherever the unicorns direct this spiralling vortex of energy, blockages are unlocked on all levels, and physical, emotional and soul healing takes place. I was keen to see how the activities of the day would lead me to an even deeper understanding of these powerful energies.

Flavia Kate had styled her long blond hair so that it cascaded down her back in long waves, reminiscent of a unicorn's mane. She radiated the pure joy and unconditional love of the unicorns and I knew instantly that here was someone who had a true connection with the unicorn frequency and who had personal inner knowledge and experience of these energies. I knew I could trust that she would interpret and translate the unicorn energy clearly and accurately into the physical realm.

Meeting My Unicorn Guide

The first meditation Flavia Kate guided us into was designed to facilitate an initial contact with the unicorns, to meet our personal unicorn guide and to learn more about their powerful healing energies. We would be flying across the globe on our unicorn guide's back and blessing areas of heavy, negative energy with silver and gold stars, representing Divine healing light, shooting from our guide's horn.

During this meditation, I met my personal unicorn guide for the first time. I had expected a graceful, delicate horse with a long, ornate, silver horn, probably influenced by childhood images and the movie *The Last Unicorn*, which was one of my favourite movies as a little girl. In the meditation, I entered a magical fairy forest where I found a circle of exuberant fairies dancing around a fire. I hid behind a tall fern and watched as they celebrated the arrival of the unicorns in their midst. Just as the merry singing, joyous clapping and ebullient dancing was at its peak, the fairy queen spotted me in my hiding place and lovingly invited me inside their circle. As the exhilarated crowd parted, I came face to face with my unicorn guide. The magnificence, joy and love of this experience took my breath away.

When I met my unicorn guide in the center of the fairy circle, I saw that he was a very big, beautiful, strong yet graceful white stallion, who seemed to be bursting with power and gentle at the same time, with a long, deep golden spiralled horn on his forehead. He told me his name was Petryxvloxitaclribilani, but that I was welcome to address him as Petruvius. Unicorn language is very complex and frequently unpronounceable to our tongues. I was told by the unicorns that words such as "we" or "you" vary greatly from sentence to sentence, depending on the meaning and context within which they are used. This is why unicorns often communicate information to us in the form of mental images, stories and visions. Often the information is encoded using symbols of the subconscious, much like dreams. Communicating with unicorns often feels similar to a shamanic vision quest, or, more prosaically, like a trip to the cinema. My guide showed me his name visually because my human hearing could not make sense of the sounds. The unicorn language seems to contain a great number of unusual (to our ears) consonant combinations. The overall impression I had of my unicorn guide was one of grace, power and pure unconditional love. Later Flavia Kate would tell us that the colour of a unicorn's horn can vary from pure white to deep gold, with the lighter end of the spectrum signifying younger unicorn souls and the deep golden horns representing the most spiritually advanced unicorn souls. Of course, even a unicorn with a white horn is still a very evolved and pure Divine being, so there is no need to be disappointed if your unicorn guide turns out to have a silver or white horn!

Next we learned about the four crystals that have a specific link with the unicorn vibration. These "unicorn stones" are Rose Quartz, Selenite, Jelly Opal and Clear Quartz. These are four very powerful crystals with unique qualities and abilities that reflect different aspects of the unicorn healing energy.

The first "unicorn jewel": Rose Quartz

Rose Quartz has a soft pink hue and is known as the Love Stone. It emits a very gentle, comforting, feminine energy. It is a stone of unconditional love that opens the heart chakra to all forms of love: self-love, family love, platonic love and romantic love. Emotionally, Rose Quartz supports gentleness, forgiveness, compassion, kindness and tolerance. Rose Quartz helps you to love and accept yourself, raising your self-esteem and sense of self-worth. It helps you release negative emotions such as fear, resentment and anger. Rose Quartz can also heal and release childhood traumas, neglect, and lack of love, by enhancing inner awareness and promoting forgiveness and self-acceptance. The heart functions as the center of all energies and unifies your being as a whole. It is the central point around which all the energies turn. An imbalance or disharmony in the heart chakra will adversely affect all the other centers. Likewise, a clearing of the heart chakra will improve the interaction of all the other centers. It is important to maintain the balanced equilibrium between all the energy centers in the body to ensure that your consciousness is adequately integrated and functions properly in your everyday life. If too much focus is given to the upper chakras, the lower energy centers lose sensitivity, vitality and function. If too much attention is given to the lower chakras, then the upper energy centers will become murky, clouded and blocked. Rose quartz assists you in finding your balance by strengthening and harmonizing the heart chakra, around which all energies revolve.

The second "unicorn jewel": Selenite

Selenite is a translucent white natural gemstone, which is also known as the Angel Stone. Translucent Selenite has a very high vibration and brings clarity of mind, rapidly opening and activating the higher energy centers of the body, in particular the third eye chakra, the crown chakra, the soul star chakra, also known as the "seat of the soul" or halo chakra, and the stellar (or star) gateway chakra. There are four transpersonal or transcendental chakras, meaning they are not located in the physical body. These are called the stellar gateway, soul star, causal chakra, and earth star.

Selenite and the Transpersonal Chakras

The soul star chakra, located about a hand's length above your head, is the energy field or portal through which the Soul braids or weaves into the physical body at the time of incarnation, and is the exit point of the soul from the body at the time of physical death. It is visualized as the "halo" in paintings of saints. The soul star chakra is formed before incarnation while we pass through the "veil of amnesia" and when activated allows our Higher Self access to the Akashic records, which is the term for the memory bank of our individual soul and the collective group soul, thereby accelerating our soul evolvement. Through meditation, this chakra becomes activated and as additional soul learning occurs, the cells and atoms of the body begin to vibrate at a higher frequency, which facilitates direct contact with the Soul and its purpose. Communication from ascended masters and higher vibrational beings with evolved consciousnesses is also facilitated by activation of this chakra. The soul star chakra is often visualized as a tunnel of pure light, or a portal, that connects the Soul to the Divine Source, or God. This Source, or God, is the ceaseless, unending, ongoing, loving, creative flow of pure conscious energy in the universe that uses change to create; an intelligent conscious organizing and re-organizing energy that runs through the whole of creation; an energy we call evolution. The evolutionary impulse of the Universe is within each one of us and we are called to evolve into ever higher levels of consciousness, individually and collectively. The soul star chakra is a brilliant, flaming white in colour. It was collectively activated during the Golden Age of Atlantis, which is so called because it was characterized by a high level of evolvement of consciousness.

The next transpersonal chakra, the Stellar (or Star) Gateway, resembles a starburst of energy and is situated at the highest point your hands can reach above your head. Its activation is experienced as a complete unification with the Divine Source. When this chakra is opened, it emits a radiant energy that looks like a swirling rainbow. We experience activation of this chakra as Oneness with Divine love, wisdom and compassion. Christ consciousness, which is also called Buddha consciousness, Krishna consciousness or Cosmic consciousness, is the realization of our Oneness with God, the truth that each of us is a conduit of Divine Mind, which is expressing and experiencing Itself through us. Because the stellar gateway chakra connects us with the Divine, it is the chakra in which all the Christ abilities lie dormant, waiting to be set free and utilized in the outer and inner worlds. It is also the location of our karmic blueprint, storing the memories, skills and abilities gained in all our lifetimes, and our life's purpose. Our planet is at this time moving towards ascension, which means there is a collective rising of consciousness towards realization of the Christ consciousness within recognition and recognition of our union with the Divine. A great deal of work and energy is at this time being sent into physical reality to help the individual open up and expand the stellar gateway chakra. The unicorns are one of the energies sent from the higher realms to assist us with the task of ascension. Selenite is helpful for purifying the Stellar Gateway.

The third transpersonal chakra, the Causal, is located behind the upper part of the skull. It is the energy center that opens to integrate the light that the upper two chakras (soul star and stellar gateway) transmit, and it assists in higher activations of the crown, brow and throat chakras, allowing us to receive Divine inspiration in these areas. You notice an opening of the causal chakra as enhanced clarity in your psychic and telepathic communications.

The fourth transpersonal chakra, the Earth Star, is the anchoring point for the powerful life force energy of our planet Earth, and is found beneath your feet. It connects you to the elemental energies of the planet, and anchors and aligns all of your chakras from the root chakra at the base of the spine to the first transpersonal chakra. This anchoring is what allows the Spirit to connect with both the Earth and Universal energies. As we are evolving in consciousness, passing through the stages of ascension, we are circulating increasingly powerful energies through our new crystalline gridwork, or lightbody. Your lightbody is a gridwork of light and sacred geometry that brings together your physical, emotional, mental and spiritual being. The sacred geometry of the lightbody is also called the "Merkaba". This is both an Egyptian and Hebrew word for the spinning field of light energy and information that radiates from the human body as the star tetrahedron, also known as the Star of David. The Merkaba is a geometrically precise field that is formed from the pattern of the first eight cells of the fertilized ovum or zygote. The location of these eight cells is in the geometrical center of the human body in the base or root chakra. These eight cells also provide the center point for all of the energy fields and grids that surround the body. Thus, the Merkaba field is the matrix of creation. Stated another way, it is the blueprint from which your physical and subtle bodies are formed and from which your life's journey and soul purpose is made manifest. As we increase the energy running through our cells, the "voltage" increases and we become more and more "electrical". For this reason, the Angels and Unicorns tell us that it is crucial that we ground ourselves and our energy in the planet's own crystalline grids, otherwise we may run the risk of blowing a few "fuses" in our system! The most effective way to ground your energy is to fully activate the Earth Star chakra. Since more than half the planet is water, the Earth Star chakra has a large "water" component and its colour is turquoise blue.

Selenite facilitates the experience of receiving advice and information from spirit guides, guardian angels and your unicorn guide in the form of "inner movies", where your guides will show you a story sequence that reveals their message symbolically. Selenite is a silica based crystal. Yogic philosophy explains that as we develop our lightbody, we move from dense, carbon based bodies of physical matter to a light, silica based light-body. Selenite regenerates cellular structures and membranes in the body, a property which makes it a powerful rejuvenator. Rubbing the crystalline structure with a finger or thumb in meditation can facilitate access to past lives as well as probable future lives. By facilitating the opening of our higher transpersonal chakras, Selenite allows us to see the inner dynamics of any situation, and live our lives in love and co-creatorship with the Divine.

The third "unicorn jewel": Jelly Opal

Jelly Opal, also known as Water Opal or Crystal Opal, is a transparent pure Opal with a gelatinous appearance and a striking opalescence, or bluish sheen. The play of colour in this stone appears as a subtle dancing gleam depending on the angle of light passing through the gem, rather than as solid colour demarcations. Jelly Opal has an other-worldly quality. It appears as a "celestial dance of light", which is barely captured and materialized in physical form. It is a very visual representation of the formless becoming form. Crystal healers and meditators use Jelly Opal as a mystical thought amplifier and as a bridge to unseen (non-physical) realms.

The fourth "unicorn jewel": Clear Quartz

Clear Quartz is known as the Master Healing Crystal because these translucent crystals function as prisms which can split light into a rainbow containing the full spectrum of colours. Archangel Raziel, whose name translates to "Secret of God", has an aura of Rainbow colours. His crystal is, of course, Clear Quartz. He helps you with dream interpretation and the recall and healing of past life memories. Archangel Raziel and Clear Quartz with its rainbow colours help heal spiritual and physical blocks. Because it contains within itself all colour frequencies, Clear Quartz has the ability to energize and rejuvenate cells of all different types and vibratory rates. It aids each cell to clear any unwanted or negative memories or patterns which may have been stored, and encourages new regenerative growth, and optimum vibratory frequency. When a cell is not vibrating at its optimum rate, dis-ease or malfunction is often the outcome. New cells are created constantly, but as they are copied as exact replicas, new cells will include any disharmonic blueprints present in the original cell. It is interesting to note that clear quartz crystals are also used in modern technological equipment such as computers, lasers, lamps and watches due to their extremely precise, accurate and stable frequencies. When cut to a consistent size and shape, quartz crystals have the ability to vibrate at thousands of times per second. The precise standard of frequency allows quartz to maintain and regulate the movement of a watch, so that it is extremely accurate. In meditation, you can experience the ability of Clear Quartz to open and activate the higher chakras, aid psychic awareness and facilitate the ability to perceive, trust and utilise subtle information or energy. This means that Clear Quartz crystals enable you to sense more clearly the reality of any given situation and what mind dynamics are at work. This understanding helps you to stay true to yourself, and supports you in living in a place of love.

The fifth "unicorn jewel": Pearl

In my communications with the unicorns, I was given the information that there is a fifth jewel that embodies the unicorn energy and that is very beneficial when attempting to establish a connection with the unicorns and in bringing their healing qualities down to earth. Unicorns love pearls, as they represent the pure, powerful, innocent white luminosity of Divine Light. Innocence in a metaphysical sense signifies truth, a complete absence of deceit or delusion. In my research, I discovered that pearls are linked with the Third Eye chakra. The unicorn horn represents the awakened or activated third eye and the unicorns feel a great affinity with the energy of pearls because they embody the same qualities of spiritual transformation, purity, faith, integrity, honesty, innocence, truth, tranquillity, wisdom and meditation. Pearls provide a clear vehicle for the advancing states of wisdom, as well as a finely tuned channel for receipt of spiritual guidance. Pearls assist you with self-acceptance. They lift your spirits and make you feel calm, poised and beautiful. They remind you to walk with Dignity. It is easy to see why the unicorns feel a close kinship with the metaphysical energy of pearls. The unicorns are visiting Earth now, to return faith and dignity to humanity. I have loved to wear pearls all my life and intuitively I can sense that their message to us is the same feeling that I have when I am in the company of the unicorns: self-empowerment, dignity, poise, calm, beauty, purity and spiritual upliftment.

How to Attract Your Own Unicorn

It is probably not surprising that all the crystals and jewels associated with the unicorns are pale, opalescent or translucent in colour. The unicorns exist on a very high, evolved frequency and they are unable to lower their vibrations in order to communicate with human beings. While angels have the ability to tune into the human experience on many levels of soul development and are thus capable of assisting people in all areas and walks of life, the unicorns can only vibrationally "find" those people who have a corresponding frequency to them. Unicorns do not have free will or free choice. Free choice means the choice to turn away from love, life, and unity; and to choose to act in ways that go against the nature of the Universe, Divine Mind, or God. Unicorns are always One with the Universal Mind, and so they are always acting from their Higher Self, or Divine Nature.

Unicorns look for people who radiate light and have a vision beyond themselves. Compassion is seen as the highest virtue in Buddhist teachings, because it is Divine love in action and it is based on a realization of unity consciousness, the knowledge that on a fundamental level we are all one. The unicorns are expressions of the unconditional love of the Divine. They wish to work together with humans who vibrate on the same frequency, who are pure of heart, who aspire to be of service to others and to make the world a better place, whether that is on a global scale or in their families and communities.

From the list of qualities associated with the "unicorn jewels", a pattern emerges that reveals exactly how the unicorns work on our vibrational force field, activate our energies and heal our body-mind. Our bodies and minds are psycho-physical units, in other words, our minds affect our bodies and our bodies in turn affect our minds. To progress spiritually, we need to open our heart chakras and express love in our lives. As I was reading through the course manual written by Flavia Kate for the Unicorn Workshop, I found that all the insights I had received during meditation were verified by what was written in here. Of course, on a deep level I had known that my experience had been valid but it was still an amazing feeling to see it all confirmed in black and white. My journey to understand the magnificent unicorn energy was only just beginning. I was going to receive much more information as the day progressed. Our next exercise would involve choosing a personal crystal from a large copper bowl filled with rose quartz hearts, jelly opal spheres, and selenite and clear quartz "eggs". My hand hovered over the bowl for a few brief seconds, as I felt instantly drawn to a smooth, opaque piece of selenite which seemed to be illumined by angelic energy.

Meditation: Meet your Unicorn Guide

Close your eyes and breathe in love, breathe out peace.

Visualize a protective white light around you or the building or place you are meditating in. You can ask Archangel Michael to help you with this. This ensures that your meditation is protected and only pure love and unicorn energy can come through.

See yourself in an enchanted forest, the full moon in the peaceful sky above you, surrounded by secret glades, large ferns and towering trees, wrapped in vines and overgrown with moss.

You hear water flowing in the distance and go to investigate. You come upon a beautiful waterfall cascading down against the backdrop of the thick forest terrain, into a large rock pool below made from many different glittering crystals, which sparkle in the moonlight. It is a scintillating sight and you feel exuberant.

As you stand mesmerized by the dance of water and the twinkling of the crystals, you see a reflection of radiant white light fall onto the still water surface. When you turn to look, you come face to face with the most magnificent creature you have ever seen. You can barely make out the shape of a unicorn in the midst of a brilliant white light. The unicorn adjusts its light to a level of brightness that is comfortable to you. Its beautiful large eyes are gazing at you with an expression of utmost love, acceptance and wisdom.

Looking into the unicorn's eyes, you make soul-to-soul contact. Listen for any messages that the unicorn may have for you.

The unicorn invites you closer. You may stroke it and hug it.

The unicorn touches your heart area with the tip of its beautiful spiralled horn. Waves of light, rainbows, and golden stars flow from the unicorn's horn, into your heart. You experience a feeling of great love, warmth and expansion. Feel the unicorn's unconditional love for you. Let it open, inspire and expand your heart.

You feel the unicorn communicating a profound truth to you. This is the love that God has for all of Creation. This is the love you feel when you are living from your true self, which is one with all of Creation, and one with God.

When you are ready, thank the unicorn and say good-bye. Now you have made a connection with your unicorn guide, you can call upon it whenever needed. The more time you spend together, the better you will get to know each other.

CHAPTER 2

Unicorn Messages

"Be patient toward all that is unsolved in your heart and try to love the questions themselves like locked rooms and like books that are written in a very foreign tongue. Do not now seek the answers, which cannot be given you because you would not be able to live them. And the point is, to live everything. Live the questions now. Perhaps you will find them gradually, without noticing it, and live along some distant day into the answer."
- Rainer Maria Rilke (Letters to a Young Poet)

Soul Purpose

When we had each chosen our crystal from the bowl, we sat down in a semi-circle with the stone between our hands. The selenite felt smooth in my hands and I could feel its energy flowing into me. In meditation, we visited our unicorn guide and asked for advice on our soul purpose and on ways in which we could be of service right now. *What is the unicorns' mission for me at this point in time? How can I best serve my fellow beings and be a light in the world right now?* In response, Petruvius looked at me with great conviction and determination and said, *"You will write a book about us."* I was completely taken aback. Although I am a writer, my articles and publications have so far centred around the topics of nutrition, pregnancy, childbirth, parenting and holistic health. I felt some internal reluctance to committing to write about "mythological creatures" and the messages they have for us. My parents are both scientists and although they are liberal Christians and hold a belief in a higher power, growing up, religion or spirituality was not a big topic of discussion in our house. Anything "New Age" was certainly frowned upon or laughed off as "the hallucinations and daydreams of those crazy hippies". Later on, as a professional, university educated person, I had not felt comfortable sharing my spiritual journey of discovery with anyone except my husband Charles, who grew up in India and has a very natural and easygoing relationship with spirituality, and a few close friends who were also interested in spiritual development, such as my friend Carrie. Now I was supposed to "go public" with my spiritual interests and write a book about my communications with the unicorns! Naturally, I responded with many questions, such as: *What will I say? How will I start? How do I do this? What exactly do you want me to write about? I don't know anything about getting a book published!* Confronted with a barrage of questions, Petruvius replied by simply nodding three times, with great emphasis (a gesture that I took as an affirmation) and mentally communicated to me: "Just start writing". When he sensed my doubt, he added, firmly: "We will help".

I was shown images of myself, surrounded by spiritual friends and sharing spiritual truth in workshops, lectures and meditation groups, travelling around the world with my work, and writing books on metaphysical topics. What the unicorns were showing me was my dream life! It was everything I had always wanted to do, but had never known how to turn into reality. I reflected back on how much I had learned in my own consciousness journey and considered how my life had changed through the application of the knowledge I had gained. I felt a great desire to share my insights with others. I remembered my near death experience three years ago, in December 2006, and how I had chosen to come back into physical existence because I felt I had so much unfinished business left on earth. I knew that I had not yet lived my life's purpose and the intention I had set for this lifetime before choosing this present incarnation. I knew that my life had been changed profoundly by my metaphysical studies, spiritual practices and meditation experiences, and now I wanted to repay my many wonderful teachers by sharing this inspiration with others.

The Elevator Question

In one spiritual development course I took we were instructed to formulate our life's purpose in form of a one-sentence mission statement. I found this exercise especially helpful. You may want to try it for yourself. For this purpose, visualize yourself taking an elevator ride with a stranger. As you stand next to each other with only a short time left before you reach your stop, the stranger turns and addresses you with the question, *"What is your intention in this life?"* What would you reply? It would have to be a short, succinct statement, summing up the aspirations of a whole lifetime in a few words, because the elevator is about to reach its destination. After some deliberation, I whittled my much longer initial response down to a brief, but to the point, mission statement: *My intention in this life is to elevate, inspire and heal people to live life authentically.*

Unicorn Inspiration

The unicorns work on the level of the soul, while the angels oversee matters of the heart. While the angels respond to people's prayers and act as Divine messengers for wishes of the heart, the unicorns tune into our soul purpose or soul longing, and enable great visions to be fulfilled. Often, soul longings are submerged in culturally or socially conditioned false selfhoods and are like a dim candle light but the unicorns recognize them and fan them with their words, or nudges, of inspiration in an attempt to turn the flickering light into a bright flame. The fact that I have written this book is proof of their powers of inspiration.

When we came out of meditation, having each received a personal message from the unicorns, we programmed the stones in our hands with the wish and intention to fulfil the mission we had been given by the unicorns. Then we formed a little procession leading out into the fairy garden, where we gently dropped our crystals into the wishing well. When it was my turn, I felt inspired to blow onto the selenite sphere before placing it into the water while fixing the vision for my life of spiritual work and service firmly in my mind. Later, during my research into the metaphysical nature of the unicorns, I discovered that the unicorns use their breath to kindle the sparks of soul desire. I realized then why I had felt nudged to use my breath to bless and activate the crystal I had programmed with my soul's purpose. The unicorns were igniting the spark (vision) of soul purpose into a blazing flame (manifestation).

Queen and Beggar Become One

After the lunch break, it was time for our unicorn healing energy system attunement. While I sat in contemplative meditation, I experienced myself walking up a wide white marble staircase, seated on the back of my unicorn guide with my guardian angel walking by my side. When I reached the top of the staircase I saw a rusty iron cage in a thicket, surrounded by brambles, wire and litter. Inside this locked cage was a figure I recognized as myself. The part of me that was seated on the unicorn's back was wearing medieval robes in violet and gold and looked and felt like a queen. In the cage was a part of me that looked bruised, pale and pained. I slowly descended from the unicorn's back and started walking towards the cage. Deep within myself, I found the power, knowledge and strength to unlock the cage, clear the debris and heal the "shadow" part of me. I set it free as a pure aspect of myself. Once freed, the person started glowing and shimmering with light. I placed my hands in the Namaste position, both hands folded above the heart, and the light person mirrored my action. The light spread to encompass us both and we merged into one. I intuitively felt that I had healed, accepted and integrated the "pain body" part of me which had been carrying all my unprocessed hurt, fear, and heart ache. My guardian angel smiled at me. I sensed that he was pleased. I asked Archangel Zadkiel, the angel of compassion and forgiveness, to transform the thicket and cage with his violet flame. As I stood watching the apparition in front of me consumed by Zadkiel's powerful violet flame, I felt deep gratitude, freedom and peace.

Archangel Zadkiel and His Violet Flame

Archangel Zadkiel is dedicated to the spiritual awakening of humanity. He is often depicted with golden wings and clothed in violet robes. The attributes associated with Archangel Zadkiel are forgiveness, mercy, transformation and freedom. The colours associated with this Archangel are violet and silver. The colour violet is the highest frequency of light that is visible to the eye and vibrates to the qualities of enlightenment, clarity and vision. It is the colour of spiritual growth and works with the highest levels of thought without using the physical senses. Silver illuminates and lights the way, reflecting like a mirror, unveiling illusions and truths. Silver is tranquil and soothes the emotions, calming and restoring harmony. The Violet Flame is one of the most powerful healing and transformational tools that we have been given by the Higher Realms to assist with humanity's evolution of consciousness. The Violet Flame is the spiritual fire of the Seventh Ray[1], known as the ray of alchemy and divine transmutation. When sunlight passes through a prism, you see it refract into seven colours: red, orange, yellow, green, blue, indigo, and violet. (In reality, the rainbow is made up of a whole continuum of colours from red to violet and even beyond the colours that the human eye can perceive.) Of the seven colours which are visible to the eye, violet emanates the most energy. In fact, the Violet Flame oscillates with such high frequencies that it not only encircles and purifies negative, lower vibrational energies, but actually transforms them into light. Zadkiel radiates the Violet Flame with pure love and intention to support our evolution into God-Consciousness. As the Violet Fire spirals energetically, it burns through the veils of amnesia, density and separation that keep us from fully experiencing our Divine nature. This flame is a gift from the Divine, and has the power to instantaneously transmute fear into love, sadness into joy, judgment into compassion, and conflict into harmony. Attuning daily to Archangel Zadkiel and the Violet Flame will strengthen your unity consciousness and allow you to live life from your authentic self, realizing yourself as an individualized expression of Universal Intelligence and a co-creator with the Divine.

The Inner Rainbow

The second half of the Unicorn Energy Healing attunement involved sitting in quiet meditation while Flavia Kate transmitted the healing

---

1   The seven rays and their Angels are: *Ray 1* Power and Will; Red; Michael. *Ray 2* Joy and Wisdom; Orange; Jophiel. *Ray 3* Love and Relationships; Yellow; Chamuel. *Ray 4* Healing, Unity, Abundance; Emerald Green; Raphael. *Ray 5* Inspiration and Clarity; Blue; Gabriel. *Ray 6* Devotion and Idealism; Indigo; Uriel. *Ray 7* Transformation and Divine Alchemy; Violet; Zadkiel.

unicorn energy to us by successively activating the unicorn energy "horns" in our third eyes and in the palms of our hands. While Flavia Kate touched my third eye and programmed my palms to open to the free flow of the unicorn healing energy, I had a vision of a white beam of light streaming down through my higher transpersonal chakras and entering my body through my crown chakra. As the white beam of light entered my crown chakra I saw it break up into the seven rainbow colours as if it had passed through a prism. I saw the energy travel down my internal body, cleansing, energising and balancing my chakras, one by one. I had a vision of my crown chakra being infused by this energy and turning a sparkling, vibrant violet. As the light travelled downwards, passing through my third eye, I saw a flash of light and then a vibrant, deep indigo colour spreading outwards. When the light reached my throat, I saw my throat chakra changing to a radiant sky blue colour. It was an extraordinary sensation, as if I was simultaneously watching the process from the outside and experiencing the cleansing from the inside. When the rainbow energy reached my heart chakra I could see that it was bright green with a few cloudy patches. The rainbow light extended to fill the entire space leaving the heart a sparkling, rich green that radiated brilliant light into the world around me. My solar plexus chakra was cleansed until it was a cheery, vibrant golden yellow colour reminiscent of the sun. The sacral chakra was purified to a glowing orange and the root chakra shone in a deep, rich red like a ruby once the unicorn rainbow energy had passed through it. It occurred to me that the rainbow light was passing through my body in a reverse mirroring movement of the *kundalini* rising in Yogic practices. Indeed, Petruvius, my unicorn guide, confirmed to me that the unicorn rainbow energy functions as a "chakra healer" and "chakra awakener" just as the *kundalini* energy does.

Kundalini: Your Life Force Energy

Kundalini is a psycho-spiritual energy, which, in its inactivated state, is said to be asleep at the lower end of the spine, in the root chakra, curled up like a snake. *Kunda* is a Sanskrit word meaning "coil" or "spiral". When *kundalini* is aroused either through spiritual discipline or spontaneously, it shoots up the spine activating the chakras in succession and thereby facilitates new states of consciousness, including mystical illumination, a recognition of the authentic self and the oneness of life. In Christianity *kundalini* is referred to as the Holy Spirit. It is the primal life force that animates all living entities, the evolutionary force behind all living matter. In Tantric Yoga *kundalini* is an aspect of *Shakti*, the divine female energy. The objective of Kundalini Yoga is to raise the *kundalini* energy to the crown chakra, where it unites with *Shiva*, or the male polarity, and inspires awakening. Intriguingly, the *kundalini* life force energy, referred to by various names, appears to be a universal phenomenon in esoteric teachings for at least the past three thousand years. *Kundalini* has been interpreted from the Bible as Christ consciousness, the recognition that we are all children of God, animated by the Holy Spirit or *kundalini*: "The spirit of God hath made me, and the breath of the Almighty hath given me life." (Job 33:4 KJV)

This life force energy is also referenced in alchemical tracts using the symbol of the philosopher's stone.[2] *Kundalini* as a spiritual experience is thought to have parallels in many of the mystical and Gnostic traditions of the world's religions, such as Quakerism, Shakerism, Judaic *Shuckling* (torso-rocking prayer), the swaying *zikr* and whirling dervish of Islam, the quiverings of the Eastern Orthodox *hesychast*, the flowing movements of *tai chi*, the ecstatic shamanic dance, the *ntum* trance dance of the !Kung Bushman, Tibetan Buddhist *tummo* heat as practised by Milarepa, the Dionysian revel

---

2   Jungian psychology equates *Kundalini* arousal with the seven stages of transmutation of metals [=activating/transmuting the seven chakras] in the attainment of the coveted Philosopher's Stone, described in ancient alchemical texts. Halligan showed how the raising of Kundalini to the crown chakra at the top of the head essentially equates with alchemical "conjunctio", the mystical marriage of opposites in any spiritual journey which makes union with the Divine a subjective reality, where the Self is fully formed. "A *conjunctio* metaphorically creates the Philosopher's Stone, the Self, unity with the Divine. Therefore, for many Jungians the experience of Kundalini awakening is the Eastern version of individuation [coming into Self-hood]." [Frederica R. Halligan and John J. Shea, *The Fires of Desire: Erotic Energies and the Spiritual Quest* (New York: Crossroads, 1992)]

of the Greek mystery schools, the Middle Eastern belly dance, and Andalusian flamenco with its Indo-Arabic spiritual origins.

In essence, *kundalini* is the primordial feminine energy of physical life. *Kundalini* is the energy released at the moment the sperm enters the ovum and which creates the flash of radiant light that the mind returns to after journeying down the tunnel of darkness at the time of physical death. It is the energy of natural child birth and for all people, the energy of the physicality of the life experience. Essentially, when your chakras are clear and vibrating at their optimal frequencies, then what you experience are the symptoms of the free flow of *kundalini,* your life force energy, as it breaks through all of the barriers that circumstances and beliefs have created.

Chakra Healing with the Unicorns

Once I had been shown how to use the unicorn's pure white light refracted as rainbow rays or light frequencies to cleanse, balance and purify my chakras I repeated the process another two or three times slowly and carefully. Each time I completed the technique, my chakras shone more brightly. I felt waves of warmth, energy and well-being pulsating through me. I was told by my unicorn guide that this Unicorn Chakra Healing Technique strengthens the upper chakras in preparation for clairvoyance, clairaudience and clairsentience. It also balances, regenerates and harmonizes all the chakral energies and subtle bodies cushioning severe nervous system reactions such as *kundalini* syndrome associated with other advanced meditation practices, making it an excellent preparation for meditation, manifestation, dream work, past life integration, clairvoyance, channelling and similar spiritual growth processes. When *kundalini* energy starts to flow abundantly in a person who has not developed or maintained a pure energy system, it can cause physical, emotional and mental problems. Common physical effects can be overheating, discomfort, exhaustion or hyperactivity. Emotional problems may show up as aggravation, depression or manic states. Mental problems may include lack of concentration or oversensitivity to surroundings. If you think you may be experiencing *kundalini* syndrome, you should temporarily stop or reduce your meditation practice, and concentrate on purification of the chakras and energy bodies. The unicorn healing energy is the perfect antidote to energy imbalances of all kinds because it is a powerful chakra purifier and balancer.

5 Causes of Energy Imbalance in the Aura, Chakras and Meridians

The unicorns want to show us how to be more in tune with our subtle energies. Our energy systems surround us, are inside of us, and pervade us completely. These energy systems include the light body, which extends beyond your aura, your aura that surrounds you and imbues your physical body, the meridian system, a system of energy channels within you in which all energy moves throughout your body, as well as the chakras, the energy transformers transmuting and processing life giving *prana* (life force) within you.

There are many issues that can affect the functioning of your aura, chakras, and meridian systems leading to a variety of physical, emotional and mental health problems. The following are five key potential issues as explained to me by the unicorns.

(1) Energy blockages, distorted auras and chakras, and holes in the aura

These can be caused by any of the following: emotions that have not been felt and released, negative thought forms absorbed from others, a view of self that holds you as separate from other people and life around you, various types of toxins (chemical, metal, pharmaceutical and others), and unprocessed past life memories or experiences.

(2) Lack of synchronization between the aura, chakras, and meridian system

These can create serious imbalances within the energy systems. Physical, emotional, intellectual or spiritual dis-ease can create imbalances in various parts of your aura, chakras and meridian system. These imbalances affect the specific chakra or meridian which in turn affects other parts of the energetic system. Nature always tries to achieve perfect balance. Any imbalance creates a disharmony in your energetic systems, resulting in distorted and out-of-sync thinking, feeling and behaviour.

(3) **Lower frequency thought forms, distorted energies and other people's low vibrations**

These can infiltrate your aura. These are a result of negative emotions, drug and alcohol abuse, environmental pollution, or lack of contact with nature such as trees, plants and flowing water. Negativity, violence and hostility in thought and behaviour in individuals, families and communities attract negative, low frequency vibrations from the wider Universe. These vibrations, thought forms and energies can have a perceptible draining effect on your vitality and energy.

(4) **Association with low frequency, low energy people**

This can result in negative energy from their aura "infecting" your aura. Energy is alive, moves around, and communicates. You can eventually become affected by the negative energy of those around you, in your home, office or community.

(5) **Underactive or overactive chakras**

These can create a variety of issues. Underactive chakras can translate into fatigue, lethargy, weight problems, or a lack of enthusiasm for life. Overactive chakras create other types of problems including hyperactivity, panic attacks, emotional imbalances and many types of health issues in the physical body such as high blood pressure.

<u>10 Signs and Symptoms of Imbalanced Energies</u>

Energetic imbalances in the chakras affect the entire body in a great number of ways. The chakras are the energetic counterpart to the endocrine system, which governs all the major vital and mental functions of the body. Of course, all physical matter is in truth a field of energy. Physical bodies are energy in dense, low frequencies. Any disbalance in the energy field will show a visible effect in the physical body or mental activity.

The following is list of ten potential effects.
1. Fatigue
2. Lacking vitality or enthusiasm for life
3. Negative, dulled or distorted thinking
4. Negative, unbalanced or confused emotions
5. Negative, unbalanced or distorted behaviour
6. Feeling disconnected from other human beings
7. Feeling disconnected from the Creator (Higher Power, Universal Intelligence, Divine Mind, God, or whatever we prefer to call our inner life force)
8. Feeling disconnected from nature
9. Panic attacks: Can be caused by a feeling of vulnerability resulting from holes in the aura.
10. Physical diseases: Correlate with a compromised energy system.

How to Treat Imbalanced Energies

Drinking vibrant clean water, physical exercise and following an organic, whole food diet can help to raise the vibration of the chakras and purify the energy bodies. One set of exercises that achieve outstanding results for activating the chakras are called the *Five Tibetan Rites*.[1] This program activates underactive chakras and is a powerful self-healing tool for any health issues you might have, including weight difficulties.

Also beneficial for cleansing and activating your energy systems are salt baths, smudging with sage, connecting with nature, and creative work such as gardening, cooking, studying, hiking, or painting. Sound and music can be used to heal the energy system. Sound can activate the chakras. There are different types of music being produced today that can activate the energy centres, which in turn activate the entire endocrine system. The Ancient Egyptians, who received their wisdom from the Atlanteans who emigrated to Egypt after the destruction of Atlantis, were aware that energetic vibration is the fundamental creative force of the universe and used vocal toning to create vowel sounds and harmonics to clear and release energy and awaken healing channels within the physical, emotional, mental and spiritual body. They also used the frequencies of gemstones for healing in the same way. Seeing a crystal healer, a Reiki (or other energy) healer, or a Unicorn or Angel therapist can be helpful for chakra cleansing and balancing to help your energy bodies and nervous centres (chakras) vibrate at their optimal frequency for the distribution and expression of *kundalini* life force.

Meditation: Unicorn Healing Light

Find a place where you are undisturbed. Sit or lie down and enter into a meditative space of being, focusing on your breathing. Allow yourself to relax.

Call a group of unicorns to surround you in a circle. Your unicorn guide may also be within the circle. The group of unicorns stands facing you. Their coats shine with a bright white light while from the life force energy horns at their third eye a rainbow-coloured energy swirls into the air around you, surrounding you with white and rainbow-coloured energy. Concentrate on breathing the energy the unicorns emanate into your being. Feel yourself being immersed in the love and light of the unicorns. If you find it difficult to feel any energy or sensations in your body then ask the unicorns to intensify their energy and to channel it into your being. Keep asking until you are aware of their presence.

With waves of energy radiating from the group of loving unicorns flowing through your being, ask them to unite and to channel their energy into your crown chakra. The unicorns will move close to you, gathering the tips of their energy horns together so they meet just above your crown chakra. A blaze of white energy will flow up into the heavens from the place that their horns meet. This light will purify all your higher chakras and higher aspects of yourself. The unicorns are focusing their minds on cleansing, activating and healing; so allow yourself to focus on being receptive to their light. A second blaze of light will allow the white light to begin to flow down into your crown chakra at the top of your head, down your chakra column and into the core and soul of Mother Earth. See the light of the unicorns continue to flow up into the heavens and down into your being at the same time. Simply continue to focus on your breathing and enjoy the sensations of pure white light running through your being, removing any negative, blocked or unwanted energy, as the white light transmutes it instantly.

Once you feel that all your chakras have been balanced and cleansed, or the cleansing process is complete, thank the unicorns and ask them to take a step back. Even when they have returned to the unicorn kingdom, the unicorn energy will remain within your being. You will feel energised, inspired and rejuvenated by their light. You can also use this visualisation or meditation to ask the unicorns to send their rainbow-coloured healing energy into your being instead of the white light energy. This meditation can be practiced every day, and is wonderful for balancing the subtle energies of your body-mind.

Unicorn Messages

The unicorns are here to show us the importance of raising our vibrations to their optimal frequency by activating all our chakras, enabling us to experience our authentic self, which is an individualized expression of All That Is. During the unicorn healing energy attunement, after I had cleansed all my chakras, one by one, multiple times, I had a vision of a powerful vortex of energy emerging from my third eye. It had a spiral cone shape and was made of golden energy extending forth and blessing everything it touched with the gift of divine love.

The unicorns are indeed messengers of divine love, here to remind us of our true nature, and our true purpose, at this crucial time in earth's history. During the attunement, I felt that I was "plugged" straight into the unicorn energy and the messages came through as clear and as vivid as watching a movie in high definition colour. The unicorns most urgently wanted to impress on me the importance of unconditional love, compassion and non-judgement, and an appreciation of nature.

In meditation, I experienced a rising of my energy frequency which caused my ego mind to dissolve. I was told and understood very clearly that living from the higher self is the only way to fulfil our true life's purpose. Our soul purpose and the reason we are here on this planet at this time is to express divine love in our own unique way.

The unicorns, the angels and all beings of higher consciousness have unconditional love and compassion for us. They know our desires, wishes and goals and they want to help us achieve them. In order to feel truly fulfilled and in control of our lives, we have to understand the basic nature of the universe and of life itself. Life is a school for the soul. It is like a game – but you need to know the rules of the game to enjoy playing it!

The Bible contains messages from beings of higher consciousness that can teach us all about "the rules of the game of life", if we understand these instructions correctly and apply them to our own life. The unicorns say that we would all be well advised to listen to Paul's advice: "Don't let the world around you squeeze you into its own mold, but let God remold your mind from within." (Rom. 12:2 Phillips) They want us to know that we are all unique incarnations of the Divine Spirit. We are, each one of us, here for a reason. The divine purpose in each of us is to love, and to express a greater degree of life. How do we accomplish that? The unicorns tell us that by getting in the flow of life, that is, coming into alignment with our authentic self, our divine nature, we free ourselves to express our unique talents and gifts which we have been endowed with by Divine Grace, to share and enrich the Allness of All That Is. Every experience, thought, and creation put forth by one of God's creations is experienced by God Itself. We are all contributing to the eternal expansion and evolvement of the Universe. All of us together have taken on the journey of Making Known the Unknown. Together, we are God, experiencing Itself, in all Its abundance, creativity and magnificence. The will of the Creator, is for us to become like the Creator, know all that can be known, and continue to Make Known the Unknown.

The unicorns say that when we understand that our divine purpose of being here is to be a revealer of divine love, then we can start to open ourselves up to God's vision for us. We can discover our own unique way to express that love and our individual mission through which we can embody that love. We become inspired by the ideas held for us in the mind of God, and they begin to live and articulate through us.

When Jesus tells us to let our light shine, this is what he means. We are to demonstrate the light of God within us, by freely and lovingly expressing the unique gifts we are endowed with by the Grace of the Most High. The feeling we have when we live in the flow of who-we-really-are is that we have come home.

CHAPTER 3

The Unicorns' Connection with the Crystal and Rainbow Children

"When it looks like the sun isn't going to shine any more, God puts a rainbow in the clouds. Each one of us has the possibility, the responsibility, the probability to be the rainbow in the clouds."
- Maya Angelou

Who are the Crystal and Rainbow Children?

The Rainbow children are a new generation of psychic, highly evolved children, who are here to help us open our hearts and progress spiritually. The Rainbow children are highly sensitive, loving, forgiving, peaceful and magical like the Crystal children. Their chakras are open, balanced and vibrant, and they emit the rainbow light frequency through their auras. The angels have said that at this crucial point of the earth's development, where we are preparing for a quantum leap in the collective level of consciousness evolution, the Rainbow children are joining us on this planet to bring the rainbow energy indoors, as many people are spending less time outdoors.

The Rainbow children have come here to bring us rainbow healing energy. Light has a healing effect and is vital for our physical and emotional well-being. In the dark winter months, many people suffer from Seasonal Affective Disorder (SAD), caused by too little sunlight. The production of the brain chemical serotonin is directly related to the degree of sunlight. Serotonin is a neurotransmitter involved in the brain's electrical communications that regulates mood, appetite, and energy levels. Serotonin cannot be stored so our brains create a fresh supply every night as we sleep. When we wake up feeling refreshed and energized, enough serotonin was produced during the night. Too little serotonin makes us feel hung-over, drained, and irritable. Carbohydrate-cravings, depression, mood swings, bed-wetting and premenstrual syndrome (PMS) may also be a sign of low serotonin levels.

Serotonin production is hindered by too little exposure to sunshine, a sedentary lifestyle, alcohol, or taking sedatives at night. When our lifestyle is imbalanced, we feel sluggish in the morning and often use caffeine and sugar to wake us up. Then, after using artificial stimulants for energy all day, we may use drugs or alcohol to fall asleep at night. This dangerous cycle of chemical dependency is all too prevalent today.

Many people do not realize that this cycle of artificially boosting and sedating the body's energy levels can trigger depression and anxiety. Often, psychoactive drugs are then prescribed which treat depression and anxiety by raising serotonin levels. Millions of adults and children take serotonin-boosting drugs such as Ritalin and Prozac, when many of them could achieve equal results without side-effects by adjusting their lifestyles and balancing serotonin levels with natural means.

Serotonin is created from sunlight by converting melatonin in the skin to serotonin in the brain. Natural ways to increase the flow and regulation of your serotonin, and improve your mood and energy levels, include choosing nourishing foods, connecting with nature, and physical activity.

The rainbow energy consists of the bands of natural sunlight which are composed of the colours red, orange, yellow, green, blue, indigo, and violet. We encounter these colours in prisms such as dewdrops and clear quartz crystals. Rainbows are associated with happiness, good fortune, and heavenly communication, because the human body was designed to absorb and assimilate rainbow energy through sunlight. We all have a rainbow inside of us, in the form of our chakras. The chakras are our connection to the Divine light, and to the physical sunlight. When we absorb sufficient sunlight and rainbow light frequencies, we feel naturally happy, vibrant and alive.

Energy healing is a way to increase your absorption of these beneficial frequencies. The rainbow energy is concentrated in Reiki, Seichim, Qi Gong, Pranic Healing, and the other names given to channeling rainbow energy through our hands and hearts. Clear quartz crystals also give us rainbow prisms by focussing and directing light into the coloured bands.

Rainbow children choose parents who know the power of love. They choose incarnations in which they are able to express their values of peace, harmony, joy, creativity and love early on. For this reason, they choose entirely peaceful and functional households. Rainbow Children are completely open-hearted and unconditionally loving. Unlike the Crystal Children who only show affection to people they trust, the Rainbow Children are universally sympathetic. They heal us with their vast heart chakras, and wrap us in a blanket of rainbow-colored energy that soothes, heals and inspires us. They are literally angels upon the earth.

My 7 year old son Kiran, born in 2002, is a Crystal Child and is featured in Doreen Virtue's book *The Crystal Children*. He has beautiful big blue eyes that appear to look straight into your soul, loves crystals, fairies and angels and has a very profound understanding of God, the Universe and his purpose in it. When he was 6 weeks old, we met a Tibetan Buddhist monk from a monastery in New Zealand at a Samhain (Halloween) celebration at the Chalice Well in Glastonbury. He asked us politely if he might be allowed to hold Kiran for a while and this tiny baby, cradled in his arms, looked straight up into the monk's eyes, perfectly serene and calm, for what seemed to be a moment suspended in eternity. It was perfectly clear that this was a wise, capable, knowing mind encased in a small, fragile body. An exchange of soul level information appeared to take place that night between the Tibetan monk and my tiny baby and I felt that the meeting had been divinely orchestrated. Intuitive people who meet my son for the first time will often spontaneously exclaim: "A Crystal child!" I took up Yoga and meditation at the age of 18, and developed an intellectual and mystical knowledge of the virtues of maitri (love) and ahimsa (non-violence, or compassion). Although I had been on a spiritual journey of discovery for years before I became pregnant, it was Kiran's birth that facilitated a powerful opening of my heart chakra.

My second son, Elias, was born in 2008. He is a Rainbow Child. Elias's story is one of perseverance against all odds.

The Story of My Rainbow Child

I was diagnosed with a malignant (cancerous) brain tumour (Grade IV medulloblastoma) in December 2006, when I was 29. Medulloblastoma is a very rare form of brain cancer. It differs from most other types of cancers in the fact that it is an embryonic development fault, in which certain brain cells do not specialize properly in the womb, leaving them open to expansive, uncontrolled growth at any future time. In other words, people with medulloblastoma are born with a ticking time bomb in their heads. There are no signs until the tumor starts to develop, and no one knows what triggers the cells to suddenly grow. I had none of the known risk factors for cancer. I have been healthy and active all my life, practicing Yoga and meditation, eating a whole food vegetarian diet for 13 years and a vegan diet for eight years before the tumor started growing.

I believe that I planned this experience before I incarnated. It was a type of "benediction by fire", where my body and surface mind were so consumed by unceasing onslaughts of pain to my physical sense awarenesses over many weeks, that I had no other option but to disassociate myself from my physical body as much as possible and go on a journey of discovery within my own consciousness. I emerged the other end, physically battered and bruised, but spiritually healed and whole. I was left with the body of a beggar and the mind of a Queen.

As I was pregnant at the time, my symptoms were initially put down to morning sickness or a "viral infection". I was experiencing excruciating migraines, nausea and dizziness, and was vomiting so severely that I lost 10 pounds in 3 days. I also completely lost my ability to walk and had to crawl on my knees if I wanted to get out of bed to visit the bathroom. I felt as though I had drunk two bottles of wine and could not stay upright, although I have never drunk that much in my life! My mother, who lives in Germany, became so worried for me that she arranged for me to be transported to her house near Frankfurt. Because flying was out of the question in the state I was in, my parents looked into hiring an ambulance helicopter but it was so expensive that they decided to make the long drive themselves. My husband drove me to France, where I was picked up by my parents together with Kiran. I have very little recollection of the twenty hour drive to my parents' house, from Calais in France to Frankfurt in Germany, except for the fact that my mother, who is a pharmacist, kept offering me anti-nausea medicine and I felt that there was no point because there would never be a time when I wouldn't feel like this! My body was so weak, after four weeks of forced bedrest and not eating due to persistent vomiting, and ravaged by such a great deal of suffering and pain that I disconnected myself from it as much as possible. My meditation practice came in very useful then, and in the six month ordeal that was to follow. The correct diagnosis was finally made on a gynaecological ward in a hospital in Germany, where I had been transferred, by a consultant gynaecologist who had the good sense (or divine inspiration) to send me for a brain scan when I started to lose consciousness. At this point it became clear to everyone that my condition was far more serious than regular "pregnancy complications" and I was rushed by emergency ambulance to a neurosurgical care unit at a large hospital in Frankfurt. Here, they immediately performed emergency surgery on me, placing a shunt to drain excess liquor from my brain which had become dangerously compressed. The tumour was in my cerebellum, near the brain stem, and it had grown so large that it was obstructing the normal flow of liquor from my brain causing it to swell. The cerebellum is also responsible for equilibrium and orientation in space, which explains my excruciating dizziness and inability to stay steady enough on my feet to be able to walk. When I arrived at the hospital, I was unconscious and in such a poor state of health that the doctors decided it would be too dangerous to give me anaesthetics, so they sat me upright and drilled a hole in my skull without any drugs. During this time, I was completely outside of my body, and the first thing I remember thinking after the operation is, "Why is somebody pulling my hair?" I was more bothered by the fact that somebody I didn't know was yanking my hair than anything else! I was completely unaware of anything that was going on in my physical environment. The doctors said I had been lucky to escape death as my brain had become so dangerously swollen that without intervention I would have very likely died within the next 24 hours. Of course, the tumour was still inside me and would continue to grow, so the momentary relief was just a brief respite before the next step.

After my condition was sufficiently stabilized, I was scheduled for a major operation, in which a surgeon would attempt to remove the tumor with the help of computerized 3D-images of the tumor location. In order to prepare for this complicated procedure, I underwent a series of test, which involved swallowing a thick tube which was inserted all the way down into my stomach. Strangely, it had an artificial banana taste which would have made me retch on its own, without a thick tube down my throat, and as I was still experiencing constant nausea, the procedure appeared to be designed to be as revolting and painful as possible for me. In hindsight, I feel that my body was taking such a battering, such an onslaught on all its senses, that I had no choice but to surrender. I kept myself in as disassociated a space as was possible, as my body appeared to be almost a foreign object, designed only for the purpose of causing me pain.

After the operation, as the drugs and anaesthesia started to wear off, I found myself dimly aware that I was in a bed being pushed along long corridors. It was like being in a movie that turns black every few seconds. I was phasing in an out of consciousness and the one clear memory I have is reading a sign that said "Intensive Care Unit" and feeling utterly confused about reality because somewhere in the back of my mind was the knowledge that I was supposed to be in Germany – so why weren't the signs written in German? My conscious mind knows that German institutions often translate important information into English, especially in metropolitan centers with a large multicultural population such as Frankfurt. But at the time I had no access to the area of my brain that stored that information and was thrown into great mental tumult. I experienced myself as in shifting, alternating parallel universes, phasing into one reality and out of the other without any conscious control.

My Near Death Experience

As I lay in my bed in the Intensive Care Unit, every inch of my body poked, pierced and prodded by injections, needles, instruments and IVs, the constant beeping and humming of a huge wall of machines behind me and a shunt connected through the skull to drain off excess liquid accumulating in my brain, I felt a strange feeling of utter calm and acceptance. I could see my body lying in the bed, in a heightened state of malfunctioning yet filled with intricately balanced, intelligent, communicating cells which were busy working at establishing a new healthy and perfect equilibrium, and I felt a surge of elation and appreciation. All of a sudden, my body seemed to dissolve completely and I found myself floating in a pure, loving, joyful universe. My mind was as expansive as the universe. It animated every particle. I was it, and at the same time, I was floating within it. I was pure awareness, pure consciousness. I was joy, peace, trust, faith, love, calm, presence, power, infinity. Time expanded so that it was multidimensional and vertical instead of linear and horizontal. Every moment was eternity and eternity was within every moment. I knew that this state of being was my True Self and that I could stay here, in perfect beauty, peace, and love, forever if I chose too. I knew that I was an immortal, infinite, eternal being, a never ending stream of consciousness that remembers everything and forgets nothing, and that physical death is not the end but only the beginning of something even greater, alive and expansive.

I thought of my sweet son Kiran, who was only four at the time, and I knew that I had to stay in a physically-focussed form to see him grow up, as I knew we had planned. I felt such a huge amount of love for him and everyone, and I knew that I had so much more left to do and to give to the world. I had assembled many skills and talents in this life and now it was time to put them to good use. I knew it was not my time to leave the earth plane; I had much more work to do. I remembered the plans I had made for this life before I was born and I was conscious of my life's purpose and what I had intended to achieve by coming here. It was a valuable, important life and I did not want to cut it short. I was not ready to leave.

I snapped back into my body, and into an ocean of pain.

Return to Physicality

I was fortunate enough to be in the care of a very skilled and compassionate neurosurgeon who was successful in removing the tumour mass without harming any of the surrounding neurological structures. All the doctors commented that it was a miracle that I didn't have any lasting neurological damage, either as a result of the long-term brain compression or as a side effect of the difficult tumor removal operation.

However, after the procedure was over I received two pieces of devastating news. The first was that I had suffered a vaginal bleed shortly after the operation was completed. I was 8 weeks pregnant at the time and had been told that there was a good likelihood of the embryo surviving the procedure. However, the bleed was not a good sign. The doctors reassured me that my HCG (pregnancy hormone) levels were still high but the bleeding continued over the next days and deep down I knew I had lost the pregnancy. Five days after the brain tumor operation that saved my life I had a dilation & curettage (D & C), the third operation in a week. After the procedure, I felt the child's spirit communicating to me, "You are not strong or healthy enough at this point in time. I will stay close. I will wait until the time is right and you and I will be able to grow me a perfect and whole body." I realized then that the baby had not been developing properly, due to the many drugs I had had to take to save my life. This understanding helped me come to terms with the loss. I could still sense the child's spirit near me, and I promised myself to nourish my body back to perfect health in order to be able to welcome this spirit earthside in vitality, peace, and joy.

My ordeal was not over yet: Tissue from my brain tumour had been sent in for laboratory testing and the results were in – I had cancer. Fourth grade cancer, to be precise; the most malignant, fastest growing and fastest spreading type. Some tumor cells had spread into other areas of my brain and could not be removed surgically because the risk of neurological damage was too high. The options that were presented to me now were chemotherapy or radiotherapy to try and target the spreading tumour cells in my brain specifically and to pre-empt the migration of tumour cells into other parts of my brain and central nervous system. After extensive research, as it was such a rare type of cancer, my doctors decided on an eight week course of radiotherapy as my best option. I was told that the treatment would significantly improve my chances of survival, but it came with a series of risks and side effects, including hair loss, neurological damage such as loss of hearing or vision problems and infertility. Needless to say, I felt I had no choice. It was a calculated risk. At this point, only the large tumor had been removed. Since it had radiated some of its malignant cells into other areas of my brain, I still had cancer. Although I was willing to do anything it took to eradicate the cancer cells from my body and survive, I was devastated at the prospect of not being able to have any more children. I felt a deep sense of yearning to be given another chance, and especially, to meet the spirit of this child that was already communicating with me in such inspiring ways.

There is no pretence in sickness. I have always been a high achiever and, as a first child, used to being in control and shouldering responsibility. Now I was completely dependent on other people. I was at my worst, without my make-up, jewellery, nice clothes, unable to pursue my postgraduate studies and run my business, and not allowed to wash my long blond hair for weeks (pieces of skull bone had to be removed during the operation to allow access to my brain so my head was covered in bandages) so that it was lank, in knots and tangles. All the external things I felt I needed to "be me" and to feel comfortable and dignified around other people had disappeared. I had to completely let go and trust in other people, and in a Higher Power. Instead of caring for others, I was in need of care. The feeling of letting go and surrendering was a struggle at first, because it felt like giving in, or admitting defeat, but when I found that place of stillness, where my conscious mind was merely witnessing events as an external observer, I found myself uplifted and carried by a power greater than myself. It was the feeling of a child who knows that an all-powerful, loving parent is taking care of their every need.

When You Change the Way You Look at Things, the Things You Look at Change

The radiotherapy treatment took eight weeks, with daily treatments. Carrie had sent me a copy of Esther and Jerry Hicks's book *Ask and It Is Given*, and I read it for inspiration every day, keeping it in my handbag, even taking it into the changing rooms in the radiotherapy unit. In this amazing, life-changing book, I found instructions on lining up vibrationally with the energy of peace and love, thereby regaining the power of my connection with Source. In this way, I was able to integrate the profound experience of my near death experience which had shown me the all-powerfulness, all-lovingness, all-expansiveness of the non-physical, with life in a physical body, with all its vulnerability, dense energy, and limitations. The teachings in this book came to me at exactly the right time and inspired me to discover the truth in the saying that "when you change the way you look at things, the things you look at change." I began to see with new eyes - the eyes of my authentic, Source-connected self - and started to realize that the radiant, abundant, prosperous world we see when we are "in the flow of things" is the world created by a Source Energy that wants us to reconnect to it and live a life of joyful well-being.

While I was lying naked on the stretcher, covered with felt tip markings, my head held in place by a painfully tight mask under the beam of an enormous, piercingly buzzing laser, and with several technicians bustling around me, I practiced gratitude. I was in a space of perfect calm. The technicians remarked that they had never seen anyone lie so still for the many minutes each treatment took. I mentally thanked the hospital staff, the technicians and the doctors for working so hard to save my life. I thanked my parents for their caring. I thanked my husband for his unwavering love and support. I thanked my son for being my inspiration and for showing me what unconditional love really is. I thanked my friends for their never ending support, streams of cards, gifts and emails. I thanked the scientists who had invented this wonderful machine which was saving my life. I affirmed the good in everything. My mind was soaring. Everyone was impressed by my positive attitude and wondered how I could be so calm and optimistic in the face of so much physical pain and an indeterminate prognosis. But the way I saw it, it was the only way. If you want to live, you have to affirm life. If you want health, you have to affirm health. If you want happiness, you have to affirm happiness. Besides, I was not going to waste any more precious life time on worrying, fretting, complaining or otherwise dispersing my energy in useless mental pursuits.

A Mermaid Without Hair

The radiotherapy treatment ended in March 2007 with the best news I could hope for: An MRI brain scan in April 2007 showed no remaining tumour cells in my brain or central nervous system. I was frail, too weak to climb stairs and had lost all of my long blond hair – but I was in remission. The medical staff tried to convince me to purchase a wig, as I had gone completely bald, but my inner voice said no. Over the course of my illness, I had learnt that my appearance was not what "made me". I had always been very attached to my long wavy blond hair. I am Pisces, so the water element is prominent in my birth chart and I have always had a great connection with water, especially oceans and beaches. My husband, a drummer, composer and producer, called his music publishing company Mermaid Records, inspired by me, because we always joked that I was a mermaid accidentally born on land. As we all know, a characterizing feature of mermaids is their long flowing hair, and I similarly felt that my hair was a marker of my identity. When it started to come out in clumps every time I brushed, I was mortified at first. Now the illness was taking the last shred of evidence of the old, familiar me, and at first I felt great resentment and a deep feeling of injustice. When I had only a few thin strands left, a change came over me. If my hair was going to fall out, I would embrace the transformation all the way. I grabbed a shaver and, looking deeply into my own eyes in the mirror, shaved my entire head. When the hair was gone, I decided to embrace its loss. With this change in attitude, I started to appreciate the feeling of liberation that came with being completely "bare". I was still me. Whatever horrors I had imagined and however much importance I had placed on my hair as a marker of who I was, it didn't matter in the end. This realization helped me on many levels. I realized what is really important, and discovered that the essence of what makes me "me" is indestructible and not tied to any external features or accessories. With this new feeling of inner strength and authentic identity, I decided to embrace my new look, put up with all the stares and show the world who I really was. This was me, right here, right now. The hair would grow again. It did, and is now thicker, glossier, and wavier than before. I'm still a mermaid after all.

Rainbow Boy

The doctors told me that the first 2 years after the cancer treatment would be crucial and that I was to have regular brain scans for the next 5 years. They also said that I could start trying for another baby in 12 months time, given that my fertility had returned by then. I spent an anxious 8 months waiting for my cycle to return, not knowing whether my fertility had been permanently damaged. The radiation treatment might have harmed my ovaries, or it might have affected the centre in the brain responsible for reproductive hormone production, or possibly both. I finally had my first period since my miscarriage in December 2006 in late August 2007. Feelings of elation, hope and deep gratitude washed over me. Now we just had to wait the remainder of the year, until the 12 month waiting period to clear my body of accumulated toxins from the cancer treatment had passed, to try again for another baby. When I found out I was pregnant again, in February 2008, I felt incredible.

From the very start of my pregnancy, the baby communicated its wishes to me. I often simply felt a sense of knowing that I had to do something and it would always turn out to be the most beneficial thing to do in the situation. Because my cancer treatment was only a year ago, the medical profession regarded me as a high risk case, but I knew that my body was healthy, strong and whole. I had no morning sickness and felt energetic and vibrant throughout the pregnancy. My first birth in 2002 had been very far removed from how I had envisioned and hoped that it would be. My own inner guidance had advised me to book a home birth but as the pregnancy progressed, I let other people's fears and opinions take over, a process which resulted in a birth which was fear-based, full of medical interventions (including four days of botched induction) and incredibly painful. Now, with this new pregnancy, I knew I would follow my inner guidance. My "benediction by fire" had given me a great deal of inner strength and an understanding of the truths and realities of life. From now on, I was going to do things My Way.

I knew immediately that I wanted to have a home water birth if I had a complication-free pregnancy. I had read all the classics on natural birth and I had all the theoretical knowledge and an intellectual belief in the ability of a woman's body to give birth naturally, gently and easily. But, with the traumatic events of Kiran's birth still lingering in every cell in my body, I knew that I'd have to go beyond an intellectual belief and understanding of the birthing process. To this end, I decided to do a hypnobirthing course. I ordered a "hypnosis for childbirth" home study course and when I was 5 months pregnant I started listening to the CDs every day. I also watched the DVDs and was greatly encouraged by the film clips of women in late stages of labour, without any signs of pain or distress, giving birth joyfully. I faithfully did the lessons, listening to the CDs and practising the techniques almost every day for the rest of my pregnancy. I also did a lot of drawing and painting, channelling my creativity into unlocking deeply held blockages, beliefs and images around birth. Every time I visualized the baby, I saw him floating in the womb, in the warm water, surrounded by a rainbow of light. I always drew him smiling, surrounded by rays of colourful light, no matter what my initial intention had been. Fascinatingly, Kiran, who was then 6 years old and who is a keen artist and loves to draw, was also producing pictures of a "rainbow baby", surrounded by rainbow coloured light, although he had never heard of the concept of Rainbow Children.

We set up a birthing pool in my kitchen in preparation for the birth. When I was in labor, I kept repeating the affirmations from the hypnobirthing course in my mind: "Your body is made to do this. Just let your body take charge. Go with the flow. Relax. Trust in the body's inherent wisdom." Every time a contraction came, I'd gently sway, breathe deeply and let the sensations wash over me without any resistance or fear. Every contraction was bringing me closer to holding my baby. Instead of resisting them, I welcomed each contraction. I climbed into the pool for the last 45 minutes of my very quick labor. I was laughing and having fun with my midwife and husband right up until the last few contractions leading into transition, at which point I felt a great urge to focus and concentrate. I went into a very deep space of connection with my Higher Self, a place of no thought, feeling the creative power of the universe pulsating through me. Charles, my husband, and my son Kiran were at the side of the pool opposite from me. They had the best view of their son and brother emerging into the world. Elias came forth into this world with a peaceful expression on his face, dreamily, eyes closed, just floating in the warm water, suspended in time. Then he flipped a somersault under water and was gently lifted up by his father. Elias's birth was an amazing, empowering and inspiring experience which fills me with the greatest joy and the deepest gratitude.

We decided to name him Elias Constantin Raphael. Elias means "the Most High", or "my God is That Which Is" (a mystic's recognition of the Oneness of God). His middle names reflect the attributes and the journey we had been on in order to welcome Elias into our family. Constantin refers to constancy, a virtue which has been very important in my life. Raphael means "God has healed" and Raphael is the Archangel of Healing. Elias, and the journey to get him here, has manifested healing in our lives.

My Rainbow boy is now one year old and has a very peaceful, calm, and self-content disposition. He radiates pure love and joy. He is beautiful, with a mop of blond hair and huge blue eyes, which look at you knowingly and with an understanding way beyond his years. He often seems to be silently amused at our antics here on planet earth and has great fun learning about our "strange habits". At 13 months of age, he can entertain himself alone for hours, and will spend great lengths of time just inspecting his hands, giggling and shrieking with delight at the wonderment of his body and the world around him. He really is a light being and his arrival has introduced the rainbow energy in the shape of increased fun, laughter, love, joy and creative expression into our lives. At the age of 32, I can say that my near-death experience, my blissful Sacred Birth experience and my unicorn attunement in meditation remain the most transformative spiritual experiences of my life to date.

Message from the Rainbow Children

It is clear to see then why the unicorns feel such a strong affinity with the Crystal and Rainbow children. Unicorns and the Crystals and Rainbows all work together with the rainbow light energy to clear and heal our chakras, balance our body-mind and help us raise our mental frequencies towards higher states of consciousness.

Those of us incarnated on planet Earth at this time are going through a time of awakening at the moment, which is going to be accelerated as the higher frequencies of the Crystals and Rainbows populate the planet, aided by the actualized consciousnesses of other species, such as the unicorns. We are heading toward a time of peace, unity, and healing. The first wave of Rainbow Children is only the beginning. As more and more people open their hearts to Divine love and actualize their Union with the Divine, the frequencies of our collective consciousness will increase and the planet will be imbued by rainbow light once again.

Unconditional love is a unifying quality of the unicorns and the Crystal and Rainbow children. They open and activate our heart chakras with their presence and energy. As their heart chakras are fully developed, expansive and open, they lead by example and show us how to express unconditional Divine love here on earth. Love is a profound and sacred force that pulls us towards deep reality. Love breaks down the ego's walls of separateness. It reconnects you with your true self. Love awakens the soul. When you fall deeply in love, you see the Beloved in the other and also within yourself. In *Dark Nights of the Soul,* Thomas Moore reminds us that: "Love has a purpose, an enormous purpose. Its task is to free you from the bubble of practicality and ordinary business, to reveal the fact that you have a soul and that life is far more mysterious than you imagined it to be."[2]

The following is a message from the Rainbow Children, given to me in November 2009:

"Just as a wave is part of the one ocean, each of us is an individual expression of the one God. As Co-Creators, each of us is the creative "heart" of this planet. You are important, and you are needed. You are a magnificent creation of the Divine Mind, utterly unique and gifted with specialized talents, skills and capabilities. The Universe loves and adores you, because it sees the Real You within you, even when it is clouded and hidden beneath the conditioned surface-mind imaginary you. The Real You is always present; just as Divine Mind is always present. You are eternally one with all of creation, because you are an individualized expression of Infinite Intelligence, just as each of us is an individualized expression of Infinite Intelligence. Love, accept and bless everyone, because to reject the minutest part of It, is to reject All of It. We, you and me, are here because we have a Divine Purpose. We are here to express and embody Divine Love (Agape). In a miraculous unfolding of events, you will discover that from this perspective, you are always on purpose and life will unfold for you in a constant stream of manifestation of all your heart desires, because what your awakened God-conscious heart desires, is the same as God's will for you!"

CHAPTER 4

Healing with the Unicorns

"A human being is part of the whole, called by us 'universe', a part limited in time and space. He experiences himself, has thoughts and feelings, as something separate from the rest: a kind of optical delusion of consciousness. This delusion is a kind of prison for us, restricting us to our desires and affection for a few nearest to us. Our task must be to free ourselves from this prison by widening our circles of compassion to embrace all living creatures and the whole of nature in its beauty."
- Albert Einstein

Only Love is Real

The unicorns are emanations of Divine Love. Love is the ultimate healer. Love conquers all. God is Love. The universe is Love. You are Love. Only Love is Real. Divine love is not to be confused with human "romantic" love. Divine love is much bigger than that. It is of a spiritual nature. It is all-encompassing, unwavering and unconditional. It always affirms Life. It creates life, sustains life, *is* life. Divine love is often attributed only to God and spiritual beings. Yet, we are all sparks of the Creator. We are emanations, outflowings, or children of the Divine. Source created each of us from the only substance it had available – Itself. The Creator is Love, we are therefore also Love. Divine Love is who you really are. In your human state, with the limited perception of your five physical senses and their immersion in materiality, it is easy to forget your true nature. You start to perceive other people, animals and nature as "separate" from yourself. However, we are all made from the same substance and are therefore all one and all connected. The ancient Vedic text, the *Isa Upanishad*, states that "all this – whatever exists in this changing universe, is pervaded by God".[3]

Quantum Physics and Unity Consciousness

Unity consciousness is confirmed on a scientific level by quantum physics, whose findings point consistently to a profound interaction between conscious mental activity and the physical world itself. The meditator's experience of a world in which the individual participates in a seamless existence, indivisibly united with the universe around him, echoes through a discovery called "Bell's Theorem".

First proposed in 1964 by the physicist John S. Bell, based on theoretical mathematical calculations, this theorem was confirmed experimentally in 1972 by Professor John Clauser at the University of California in Berkeley. It has turned modern western science on its head and has shown the limitations of the rational, logical mind to comprehend the reality of the world around us. Henry Stapp, professor of physics at Berkeley, has called it "the most important discovery in the history of science".[4] In a nutshell, Bell's Theorem states that, "If the statistical predictions of quantum theory are true, an objective universe is incompatible with the law of local causes".

An "objective universe" is one that exists apart from, or outside of, our consciousness. The term "law of local causes" refers to the assumption that events in the universe occur at speeds which do not exceed the speed of light. This limitation, specified in Einstein's special theory of relativity (1905), is a central tenet of the modern theory of physics. In 1935, thirty years after formulating his influential special theory of relativity, Albert Einstein, using mathematical reasoning, proposed the idea that, if quantum theory were accurate, "a change in the spin of one particle in a two particle system would affect its twin simultaneously, even if the two had been widely separated in the meantime". The controversial nature of this statement hinged on his use of the word "simultaneous", which was in direct contradiction to his own special theory of relativity, which forbids the transmission of any signal faster than the speed of light. Obviously, in order to communicate to a particle "how to behave", a signal will have to travel faster than the speed of light if instantaneous changes are to occur between the two particles.

Bell's Theorem proves that Einstein's "impossible" proposition does in fact hold true. Instantaneous changes in widely separated systems do occur. When experiments verified the mathematical calculations supporting this theorem, physics (and all of modern scientific research and philosophy) had to re-think its own foundations. Mathematics and experimentation have brought modern science to the final frontier, beyond which the logical mind cannot go. Contemplate this: two particles once in contact, separated even to the furthest reaches of the universe, change *instantaneously* when a change in one of them occurs!

Naturally, physicists are attempting to find explanations for these "unthinkable" processes. One theory is that, in some (as yet) unexplainable way, the separated particles are still in contact with each other although isolated in space. In 1979, French physicist Bernard d'Espagnat stated his perception of quantum reality in words that echo the mystical experiences of unity and oneness of meditators throughout the ages: "The entire notion of an external, fixed, objective world now lies in conflict not only with quantum theory, but in facts drawn from actual experiments ... in some sense all these objects constitute an indivisible whole".[5]

As above, so below. Universal principles that apply in the invisible world of the atom are mirrored in our microcosmic existence. The oneness that is implicit in Bell's Theorem applies to human beings and atoms alike. The interrelatedness of human consciousness and the world we perceive is obvious in Bell's Theorem. Human consciousness and the physical world can no longer be regarded as distinct, separate entities. What we call physical reality, the external world, is shaped by human thought. We are intimately connected not only with the people we live with and the planet we live on, but with the farthest expanses of the cosmos.

The Universe as Hologram

A new revolutionary thought in quantum physics states that *each part* of the universe contains all the information present in the entire cosmos itself. This concept is similar to a giant oak tree producing an acorn that contains all the information necessary to replicate itself, or a set of Russian Dolls, in which each doll contains within it an exact replication of itself. This assertion is so mind-boggling in the field of science, even within the logic-defying realms of quantum physics, that nobody in the field would give it serious consideration if it had not been proposed by David Bohm, who worked closely with Einstein at Princeton University, and is considered one of the pre-eminent theoretical physicists of our times.

Bohm put forth the radical proposal that the reason subatomic particles are able to remain in contact with one another regardless of the distance separating them is not because they are sending a mysterious, unidentified signal back and forth - that would be breaking all known physical laws as it would have to be travelling faster than the speed of light - but because their separateness is an illusion. At a deep level of reality the particles are not individual entities, but extensions of the same fundamental substance.

Hologram is derived from the Greek words for "whole" and "message", and literally translates to "the whole (or complete) message". A hologram is a specially constructed image which, when illuminated by a laser beam, appears suspended in three dimensional space.

To make a hologram, the object to be photographed is first bathed in the light of a laser beam. A second laser beam is bounced off the reflected light of the first and the resulting interference pattern (the area where the two laser beams intermingle) is captured on film. The developed film looks like a meaningless swirl of light and dark lines. But as soon as it is illuminated by another laser beam, a three-dimensional image of the original object appears. The three-dimensionality of such images is not the only remarkable characteristic of holograms. If a hologram of a rose is cut in two parts and then illuminated by a laser, each half will still be found to contain the intact image of the rose. Even if the halves are divided again, each snippet of film will always be found to contain a smaller but complete version of the original image. Unlike ordinary photographs, every part of a hologram contains all the information possessed by the whole.

Only temporally and spatially coherent light will reveal the holographic images. Coherent light is defined as light waves that are "in phase" with one another. This means that the crests and troughs of the waves are aligned or matched up. Light produced by lasers is coherent light. Light from light bulbs or the sun, however, is incoherent light.

In holograms, the information of the whole is contained within each part. The entire representation of the original object is contained in each portion of the hologram. Bohm came to the conclusion that the same principle can be applied to the universe as a whole, that the universe itself is constructed as a hologram. For Bohm, order and unity proliferate throughout the universe in a way that is hidden from our physical senses, in the same way that order and organisation pervade throughout the hologram. Each part of the universe contains enough information to reconstitute the whole. The form and structure of the entire universe is held, or embraced, within each part.

It sometimes appears that quantum physics deals exclusively with the smallest building blocks of the universe such as electrons, protons, strings or quarks whereas relativity theory is concerned with gigantic objects of cosmic proportions such as stars, galaxies, or black holes. But the holographic universe theory explains that we are intricately linked to *all* of these phenomena. Ultimately the entire universe with all its "particles" including those constituting human beings, their laboratories, and their observing instruments has to be understood as a single undivided whole, in which analysis of separately and independently existent parts has no fundamental reality.

The Holonomic Model of the Brain

In meditation, we experience ourselves as one with the universe and one with universal consciousness. Science has now reached a point when its findings are echoing the meditator's direct experience of the ultimate nature of reality. What are the implications of a scientific theory of a holographic universe? As part of the universe, do we have holographic features ourselves that allow us to comprehend a holographic universe? This is exactly what the holonomic brain theory suggests. In essence, the brain is the "photographic plate" on which information in the universe is encoded.

In collaboration with Stanford neuroscientist Karl Pribram, Bohm helped establish the foundation for Pribram's theory that the human brain operates in a manner similar to a hologram, in accordance with quantum mathematical principles and the characteristics of wave patterns. The holonomic model of the brain developed by Pribram and Bohm describes a "lens defined" world view, meaning that you perceive the universe through the filter of your own mind and therefore create your own reality. In other words, things – people, events, circumstances – are not outside of you, existing as a distinct, separate, objective reality, but are created *in your mind*, filtered through your senses and given form by your thoughts. In this way, everyone will have a different world view and perceive things differently, even if looking at the exact same object. Everyone has a unique lens, which is unlike any other, created and constantly changing as a result of individual life experience, beliefs and thoughts. The rainbow, which is the result of the refraction or "splitting" of white light through a prism, is a symbol for the diversity (colours) that arises from oneness (white light). Seen this way, sameness is not desirable – can you imagine a rainbow without colours? We waste a lot of energy on trying to get others to agree with us, to conform to one "right" way of living, believing, and being -- when life was never designed to be that way.

Bohm gave the following illustration to help us visualize the way he thinks the universe and our mind works:

"Imagine an aquarium containing a fish. Imagine also that you are unable to see the aquarium directly and your knowledge about it and what it contains comes from two television cameras, one directed at the aquarium's front and the other directed at its side. As you stare at the two television monitors, you might assume that the fish on each of the screens are separate entities. After all, because the cameras are set at different angles, each of the images will be slightly different. But as you continue to watch the two fish, you will eventually become aware that there is a certain relationship between them. When one turns, the other also makes a slightly different but corresponding turn; when one faces the front, the other always faces toward the side. If you remain unaware of the full scope of the situation, you might even conclude that the fish must be instantaneously communicating with one another, but this is clearly not the case."[6]

Note that in this example no viewpoint can be said to be "better" or "more right" than the other. Both realities are correct in their own way, viewed from their own angle and their own perspective of perception. In fact, together they add up to a more complete picture of what is happening within the tank. It is the same way with our life experiences. Together, all the different thoughts, beliefs and events experienced by every single individual – every individuated stream of consciousness – add up to form a greater, more colourful and more expanded whole. Together, we are universal consciousness, experiencing Itself in us, as us and through us – forever expanding, forever learning, forever evolving into the unknown; forever *becoming* more.

The "Holoverse" and the Fourth Dimension

The same principle of indivisibility also applies fundamentally to space and time. We perceive the space around us as three-dimensional. According to Einstein's theory of relativity, time and space are inseparably linked. Adding the time axis to our three-dimensional space makes our space-time-continuum four-dimensional. For this reason, time is often referred to as the "fourth dimension".

Recall Bell's theorem involving non-local features of the universe and its finding that objects once in contact, though separated spatially, even if placed at distant ends of the universe, are somehow in inseverable contact, with any change in one of the "twins" instantaneously causing the other to change in a like manner, implying that any information transmitted between the two particles travels much faster than the speed of light. Since it is impossible for anything to travel faster than the speed of light, according to the special theory of relativity, this communication is said to be non-causal, which means that it is not caused by the transfer of any conceivable kind of energy passing between the two far away objects. Now, if time and space are inseparable, then, although these non-local and non-causal descriptions are worked out for objects separated in space, the implications of quantum theory must likewise apply to moments in "time". The sacred Hindu scripture *Bhagavad Gita* says: "Without and within all beings the unmoving and also the moving; because of Its subtlety, unknowable; and near and far away is That [Source, God, Universal Consciousness]".[7]

According to Bohm, the apparent faster-than-light communication between subatomic particles is really evidence that there is a deeper level of reality we cannot penetrate, a more complex dimension beyond our own. We view objects such as subatomic particles as separate from one another because we are seeing only a portion of their reality. Such particles are not separate "parts", but facets of a deeper and more underlying unity that is ultimately as holographic and indivisible as the previously mentioned rose. And since everything in physical reality is comprised of these "eidolons" (images or phantoms), the universe is itself a projection, a hologram.

If the apparent separateness of subatomic particles is illusory, it means that at a deeper level of reality all things in the universe are infinitely interconnected. This is also known as entanglement theory. It accounts for simultaneous phenomena in nature, such as when all birds migrate together, not one by one. The electrons in a carbon atom in the human brain are connected to the subatomic particles that comprise every dolphin that swims, every heart that beats, and every star that sparkles in the sky.

Everything interpenetrates everything, and although the left-brain function of human consciousness may seek to categorize and pigeonhole and subdivide the various phenomena of the universe, all apportionments are necessarily artificial and all of nature is ultimately a unified, interlinked, continuous web.

In a holographic universe, even time and space can no longer be viewed as fundamentals. Because concepts such as location break down in a universe in which nothing is truly separate from anything else, time and three-dimensional space, like the images of the fish on the TV monitors, would also have to be viewed as projections of this deeper order.

At its deeper level, reality is a kind of superhologram in which the past, present, and future all exist simultaneously. This suggests that given the proper tools it might even be possible to reach into the superholographic level of reality and at will draw out scenes from the long-forgotten past.

Psychics and mystics are already demonstrating this ability. Famous psychics such as Edgar Cayce, the "sleeping prophet", seem – when in altered states of consciousness – to have a direct, open line to this universal storehouse of information, enabling them to pull up information from a vast library containing the collective history of humankind as well as the individual histories of "entities", individuated streams of consciousness which we perceive as individual human beings. The holographic theory of the universe and of the mind suggests that in our own minds lies the same potential, as evidenced by spontaneous or voluntarily induced past life regressions experienced by individuals in altered states of consciousness such as in meditation, the dream state or under self-hypnosis.

If the superhologram is the matrix that has given birth to everything in our universe, at the very least it contains every subatomic particle that has been or will be – every configuration of matter and energy that is possible, from snowflakes to galaxies, from blue whales to gamma rays. It must be seen as a cosmic storehouse of *All That Is*. As the Infinite knows no time constraints, the present moment contains all that has been and will be, in eternity.

Together, the ideas of Bohm and Pribram create a new model of the human being: you use a brain that encodes information holographically and it is a hologram that is a part of an even larger hologram – the universe itself.

"Ho'oponopono": Love Heals

We know from life experience, and quantum physics has proven on a scientific level, that the mental activity of consciousness exerts measurable effects on the physical world, including human bodies, organs, tissues, and cells. In this way, we find that mind becomes a legitimate factor in the unfolding of health and disease. Your physical body has more cells in it than there are stars in the galaxy, and every cell coordinates its activity all at once with all the other cells. Information between cells can be transmitted instantaneously, faster than the speed of light. Your body can do so many things at once.

Thomas Edison, who invented the lightbulb, said: "The doctor of the future will give no medicine." This means that the healer understands that the mind and body are able to conjure and orchestrate vast inner resources and the most valuable service a physician can provide is helping to maximise a patient's recuperative and healing potentialities. One of the greatest healers of the 20th century, Nobel laureate Albert Schweitzer (1875-1965), a physician, theologian and philosopher, said: "Each person carries his own doctor inside him. They come to us not knowing that truth. We are at our best when we give the doctor who resides within each patient a chance to go to work."

A Course in Miracles states: "A sense of separation from God is the only lack you really need to correct."[8] Ultimately, the illusion of separation is the only thing we ever have to heal. The direct antidote to a sense of separation is divine love. This is the secret behind the fact that love is the ultimate healer. When we realize that All Is One, we transcend the limited confines of the intellect, and enter into a wider expansive awareness that integrates, supports and recognizes the psycho-physical processes of our bodymind. In the spiritual culture of the native Hawaiians, love is realized as the fundamental healing principle in a practice called Ho'oponopono. Ho'oponopono is an ancient Hawaiian practice of reconciliation and forgiveness. Similar forgiveness practices were performed on islands throughout the South Pacific, including Samoa, Tahiti and New Zealand. Traditionally, Ho'oponopono is practiced by healing priests or *kahuna lapa'au* (physicians) among family members of a person who is physically ill. Modern versions of the healing practice are performed within the family by a family elder, or by the individual alone. Simply put, ho'oponopono means, "to make right", or "to rectify an error". According to the ancient Hawaiians, error arises from thoughts that are tainted by painful memories from the past. Ho'oponopono offers a way to release the energy of these painful thoughts, or errors, which cause imbalance and disease.

Dr. Ihaleakala Hew Len, a Ho'oponopono practitioner and educator explains the process like this:

"Ho'oponopono is really very simple. For the ancient Hawaiians, all problems begin as thought. But having a thought is not the problem. So what's the problem? The problem is that all our thoughts are imbued with painful memories, memories of persons, places, or things. The intellect working alone can't solve these problems, because the intellect only manages. Managing things is no way to solve problems. You want to let them go! When you do Ho'oponopono, what happens is that the Divinity takes the painful thought and neutralizes or purifies it. You don't purify the person, place, or thing. You neutralize the energy you associate with that person, place, or thing. So the first stage of Ho'oponopono is the purification of that energy. Now something wonderful happens. Not only does that energy get neutralized; it also gets released, so there's a brand new slate. Buddhists call it the Void. The final step is that you allow the Divinity to come in and fill the void with light. To do Ho'oponopono, you don't have to know what the problem or error is. All you have to do is notice any problem you are experiencing physically, mentally, emotionally, whatever. Once you notice, your responsibility is to immediately begin to clean, to say, 'I'm sorry. Please forgive me.'

So how do I get that across to people — that we are each 100% responsible for problems? If you want to solve a problem, no matter what kind of problem, work on yourself. If the problem is with another person, for example, just ask yourself, 'What's going on *in me* that's causing this person to bug me?' It's simple: 'I'm sorry for whatever's going on. Please forgive me.'

The intellect is so picayunish in its way of solving problems! It doesn't realize that when a problem is solved by transmutation — by using Ho'oponopono or related processes — then the problem and *everything related to it* is solved, even at microscopic levels and back to the beginning of time."[9]

Hawaiian spirituality teaches the three parts of the self, which are the key to self identity. These three parts — which exist in every molecule of reality — are called the Unihipili (child, or subconscious), the Uhane (mother, or conscious), and the Aumakua (father, or superconscious). When this "inner family" is in alignment, you are in rhythm with the Divinity. With this balance, life begins to flow. Thus, Ho'oponopono helps restore balance in the individual first, and then, as a result, because everything is interconnected, in all of creation.

All healing is ultimately based on the principle of re-aligning with who-you-really-are. It is a challenge to accept 100% responsibility for everything in your life, including your physical state, but what this really means is that *you are in control*. You cannot control others and their thoughts, beliefs and creations because that would defy the law of free will. You *can* control your own thoughts. You can create any condition you desire through your thoughts. Any thought that is not based on love (the fundamental principle of the universe) a thought of separation, lack and pain. You always know wheth thought is constructive or destructive, positive or negative, ali with love (and truth) or aligned with separation (and delusion) way you feel. Your feelings are the ever-present guides given by the power that created you to help you on the journey life authentically. When you view life through the eyes of S Creator, you feel joyful, creative and inspired. When yo thoughts that are unloving, judgmental or otherwise d form who-you-really-are, you never feel good.

Many therapists – psychiatrists, psychologist, c even spiritual healers – still work from the assum are working on their client, "fixing" or healing l love understands the interconnectedness of all th heal another if you heal yourself first. If therapy that it is your job to save the other person, heal the other person or guide the other person, then any guidance you give will come from the intellect, your rational mind. The intellect is your surface mind. By its very nature, it does not have access to deeper levels of understanding where problems come from and how to approach them.

In Ho'oponopono, when a patient follows their physician's or healer's instructions and takes a specific medication or herbal remedy for their problem, but it does not work for them, the practitioner would approach the question from their own perspective, asking "What is going on *in me* that this woman is experiencing this herb not working for her?" After receiving information from the Divinity, their Higher Self within, the Ho'oponopono practitioner will then work on whatever arises as a response to that question *within themselves*.

Dr. Ihaleakala Hew Len is an inspiring example of the true power of ho'oponopono and divine love. Working as a staff psychologist at Hawaii State Hospital for the Criminally Insane, when he first started working there, the ward for criminals was full of violence. When he left four years later, there was none. How did he accomplish this amazing feat? Astonishingly, he did not even communicate directly with the inmates. He explains: "Basically, I took 100% responsibility. I just worked on myself. I would only go into the building to check the results. If they still looked depressed, then I'd work on myself some more."[10]

Divine Love is all-powerful, life-giving and limitlessly creative. All life originates in love, is created out of love, is born out of love. When life moves away from its Source, Divine Love, by wrongful thinking and "error", it becomes like a fish out of water or a plant without soil – unnourished, imbalanced, and dis-eased.

The unicorns, as embodiments of Divine Love, are powerful healers. They heal through love, correcting all misperception, confusion and error in your thinking. Love is ultimately the only thing that ever heals. We can only be *loved* into alignment with our true nature, our God consciousness, not forced, punished or coerced. The unicorns assist you towards self-acceptance through complete non-judgment, patiently loving you into a consciousness of unity, and in the process freeing you to live life from your authentic self.

How to Bring Your Thoughts into Alignment with Who-You-Really-Are

The best way to bring healing to every part of your life — and to the entire universe — is to take 100% responsibility and work on *yourself.* Self-care is a simple wisdom but a powerful concept.

The unicorns advise me: *"Take good care of yourself. If you do, all will benefit".*

The following are "thought control" practices given to me by the unicorns to assist with physical, personal and global healing. Remember, we are all interrelated so any healing you achieve for yourself will be passed on to the entire universe on some level.

Steps to Thought Mastery:
Change Your Thoughts, Change Your Life

1. Become aware that you are thinking.
2. Be aware of every thought you are thinking.
3. Learn to divide your mind into two parts: the thinking aspect and an "observing awareness".
4. Screen your thoughts with the "observing awareness" and accept or reject every thought. Remember: Only Love is Real. Reject any thought that contradicts Love – make sure that what you are thinking affirms connectedness, harmony and peace.
5. Every time you think an unkind thought about somebody, affirm: "My higher awareness guides me to an understanding of why they are the way they are, and through understanding I bless them."
6. If you find it hard to bless someone due to ongoing resentment, affirm: "I call upon the Higher God-Self within me to forgive the person who I currently do not seem to have the power to forgive."
7. There is a positive and a negative side to every person and thing. Always affirm and acknowledge the positive.

If you cannot find anything positive, think about something else to be grateful for. Gratitude is an instant antidote to mental negativity of all kinds.

8. Always be aware of how your thoughts are affecting you. Every thought you have creates and shapes your reality. Your thoughts have the power to clear up any problems, or to magnify them and attract more of them to you.

9. *Everything* starts in the mind. Through your thoughts, you are a Co-Creator with Universal Mind.

10. In the absence of any negative thoughts, your mind returns to its natural positive state.

Remember that the universe *always says yes*. The universe is perfectly inclusive. It rejects nothing. Whatever you are thinking, the universe agrees with you. So, if you think "I don't have enough money", then the universe affirms that you don't have enough money and will bring more "not enough money" situations into your experience. If you say "I am unwell", the universe agrees with you and you will attract more "unwell" conditions. When talking or thinking about your life, only affirm conditions that you *do* want to experience. Instead of "I don't have enough money" think "I have enough money to pay for everything I need". Rather than "I am unwell" say "I am getting better" and picture yourself in perfect health.

What you see inside your mind today is what you will see on the outside tomorrow. To operate this law of visualization you must dream, you must visualise, you must engage your imagination. It is a law — "as a man thinketh in his heart so is he" (Proverbs 23:7). Your mind is the film in the camera. Whatever image is printed on the film is what will be printed out for you on the photo. The same principle applies to your mind. The same principle applies to that picture inside you. Life will always "print" or manifest the picture inside you. There is an invisible power that prints out the picture that is in your heart, so to change your life, you must change your thoughts. Change your vision. It may feel like you are pretending and not facing reality, but *there is no reality aside from the one you create.* What you are really doing when you change your perception towards the wanted is recognizing the holographic nature of your mind. You are the creator of your own experience. When you change what you perceive, what you perceive changes.

CHAPTER 5

Learning to Express Divine Love with the Unicorns

Teach only Love,
For that is what you are.
- A Course In Miracles

<u>You Are Love</u>

Edgar Cayce, in a reading given in 1941, expressed the profound truth that All Is Love and that we are all interconnected, therefore the experience of a single individual affects the Whole:

"For, as it remains to this present day: That declaration made and those influences entertained, whether for construction or destruction, depend upon the spirit with which the declaration was made. In other words, with what spirit do ye declare thyself? That in conformity with the universal consciousness, the law of love? Or that of hate, dissension, contention – which brings or produce burdens upon thy fellow associates? For the law of love is unchangeable; in that as ye do it to the least of thy fellows, ye do it to thy Maker."[11]

As far as we can see, there are two basic divisions in the universe – consciousness and matter. Matter, or physicality, is all that we can see around us of which everything in the manifest Universe is made including our own bodies. Einstein has proven that matter is in truth a form of energy. Mystics, hermetics and metaphysicians have long known from direct experience in meditation what science has now proven. There is only one fundamental substance in the universe. Matter and consciousness are differences of degrees of vibration, not differences of substance. Matter is a manifestation of Infinite Intelligence or the creative forces of the universe known as "The All" in hermetic writings.[3] All of manifested creation solely exists within The Mind of The All, or God. For this reason, matter is subject to the will and laws of the Infinite in its aspect of manifested being.

As we have seen, science has already established the fact that there is no such thing as a "solid object". Quantum physics has shown that atoms behave as though they are intelligent because they are able to communicate with each other across vast distances. Each atom knows its place in the order of things. Atoms do not only behave as particles but as wave forms of energy as well. When an atom behaves as a wave form it contains all that one can scientifically know of the particle, both its position and its speed. But, instead of being able to predict the positions and speeds of particles, all that physicists can predict scientifically is the wave function. This means that science can predict only half what it could, according to the classical nineteenth century measurements, which are attributes (dependents) of the spacetime continuum.

Even when an atom manifests as a particle, it is still not as "material" as it appears to us because sometimes it is in two places at the same time. There are quantum leaps. This is when subatomic

---

3   Hermetics or the Western Hermetic Tradition is a set of philosophical and mystical teachings based primarily upon the Hellenistic Egyptian writings attributed to Hermes Trismegistus (meaning "Thrice Great") who is linked with the Egyptian god of writing and mysticism Thoth and the Greek messenger deity Hermes. The term *Hermetic* comes from medieval Latin *hermeticus*, which in turn is derived from the name of the Greek god Hermes. In Hermetic philosophy the supreme Principle is referred to variously as 'God', 'The All', or 'The One'. *The Emerald Tablet of Hermes Trismegistus* is a short work which coins the well known metaphysical principle "As above, so below". The actual text of this maxim, as translated by Dennis W. Hauck reads, "That which is Below corresponds to that which is Above, and that which is Above corresponds to that which is Below, to accomplish the miracle of the One Thing". Other important hermetic texts are the *Kybalion* and the *Corpus Hermeticum*.

particles move from one place to another without passing through the space between, like the "beaming up" mechanism in the science fiction series "Star Trek". Finally, there is the "observer effect" which reveals that the physical universe does not exist unless a conscious being is looking at it. Not only does the act of perceiving create physicality in the first place, but, fascinatingly, particles behave differently just by being observed.

There is a field of uncertainty where the laws of nature are not scientifically predictable any more. Stephen Hawking remarked, "Not only does God definitely play dice, but He sometimes confuses us by throwing them where they can't be seen",[12] meaning that the human intellect cannot possibly explain everything. There is uncertainty. As Hawking says, "God still has a few tricks up his sleeve". What uncertainty means for us is that life works on the basis of potentiality. In other words, we create our life through the choices we make. At every point in time there is the potential for certain choices and outcomes and by creating or choosing a cause, we are simultaneously creating or choosing the related outcome. This can be as simple as choosing where to go on holiday. If you make a choice to go to the Florida Keys then you will book a flight and accommodation on the Florida Keys, and not in Mexico or France, for example. By making this one choice another series of choices will be presented to you, which is different from the sequence of choices that would have been available had you chosen to go to France, or stayed at home. In quantum terms, by making one choice you are collapsing all other parallel universes that represent the other potentialities, or choices, that you could have lived.

All choice is first and foremost thought. By controlling your thoughts, you control your choices, and in turn your experiences. Even the physical structure that executes your thoughts on a material plane, your brain, is subject to the influence of mind. The brain is not a fixed structure. There is neuroplasticity, which means that it is malleable. Thoughts and acts of compassion, joy, and loving kindness change the structure of the brain. Positive thoughts and thoughts of love can change your brain and your physical make-up (your genes).

The wave forms of atoms are non-material by nature. They are manifestations of infinite consciousness, a non-local, non-causal field of intelligence that science knows very little about at the moment. In its creative aspect, Infinite Mind, The All, God or Universal Consciousness generates enormous waves of vibratory energy through the effort of its will and manifests the sub-atomic and atomic particles of which all manifested matter in the Universe is made. It does not discriminate between beliefs, skin colour, social status, religion, government, or nation. It does not favour anybody or anything. It is unconditional in the manifestation of Life and the Love it has for its Creation.

There is only one substance in the universe. Everything manifest and unmanifest is created from that one substance. That includes you and me. Pure Divine Love is what we all are. Regardless of appearances and behaviours, each individual's existence is birthed out of Love. Each of us has their cause and source in Love. The dynamic life force of Love is our true lineage and core essence. From this core essence, or first cause, the apparent dual nature of Creation emerges. Through the highest frequency waves of sound and light the Unified Consciousness flows forth and forms the archetypes of divine masculine and divine feminine. A polarity is established. The yin-yang symbol is a visual representation of the polarity of the manifest universe — masculine-feminine, positive-negative, white-black, solid-fluid, up-down, past-future, pushing-yielding, and so on. Every force has an opposing, or complementing, force. As this cosmic dance continues myriad "birthing" of Soul, individuated streams of consciousness, occurs and recurs endlessly.

Today, at this time in the evolutionary continuum, we are re-awakening to our true essence and nature, and freeing ourselves from our self-inflicted programming, conditioning and limitations. We are becoming Divine again through the activity of becoming fully human. As you wake up to your true nature and re-connect with your God-consciousness, you become first a pure channel and then an embodiment of Divine Love. This is a natural progression. The difference is one of degree. As you mature in the spiritual growth process, you pass through different stages of consciousness. Think of a large body of water, like a lake or ocean. When there is a storm, the waves are fierce, erratic and destructive. When the weather is calm, the surface of the water is perfectly still, like a mirror. Likewise, when you calm the chaotic waves of your intellect and see your conditioned ego-mind consciousness for what it really is, a figment of your imagination, your mind becomes a clear mirror of the Divine.

The Four Stages of Spiritual Growth

The four phases of spiritual growth in consciousness are the victim consciousness, the manifestation consciousness, the channel consciousness, and the beingness consciousness. When you are in the first stage, acting from a victim consciousness, you think that there is a barrier between you and the world outside, you project yourself as separate from everybody and everything around you and you believe that external factors are determining your destiny. This has the effect that your life feels beyond your control, it is happening to you and you are on this wild rise without influence or a steering wheel. As a consequence, you blame outside factors such as people, events, and circumstances, for your experiences. You believe that you are not consciously choosing your life, but rather, you act and re-act on the basis of hidden, unconscious, and (socially and culturally) conditioned beliefs.

In the second phase, you have understood more about the laws of life and you have become a conscious manifester, or deliberate creator. You take more responsibility and understand that your thoughts are things; they become your experience. By controlling and directing your thoughts, you manifest your visions and determine the course of your life. In the third stage, the Channel stage, you become an opening for a Higher Power to go through you.

Then, when you gain a broader perspective on life, you realize that the purpose of life is not to be found in following the guidance and desires of your ego-mind. You instinctively grasp that there is more to who-you-are, and a deeper meaning to life. In this way, you reach the channeling stage of consciousness, where you surrender the ego-self to a higher vision of yourself.

Finally, in the last phase, the state of Beingness, you feel that you are one with the Creative Force, or Higher Power. It is not just flowing through you. You are not merely channeling it. Instead, you recognize and accept that you are it. You surrender to it and become it, by acknowledging what you have been all along.

These stages are not contradictions. They are merely phases of consciousness. Napoleon Hill, author of *Think and Grow Rich*, asserted: "Whatever the mind can conceive and *believe,* it can achieve".[13] If you long for this to take place at the highest level, you have to surrender the ego-self and live life from a broader perspective, and accept yourself for what you truly are, as a co-creator with the Divine. The thirteenth century mystic and teacher Meister Eckhart explains this profound concept with the following words:

"God does not ask anything else except that you let yourself go and let God be God in you. The seed of God is in us...now the seed of a pear tree grows into a pear tree, and a hazel seed into a hazel tree, the seed of God into God. God's ground is my ground and my ground is God's ground. Here I live in my own. All of our works should grow out of this innermost ground without a why or wherefore. Then, God and the soul do one work together eternally and very fruitfully. Then all that this person works, God works... and just as I can do almost nothing without God, so too God can accomplish nothing without me."[14]

With manifestation consciousness, you are aware that you are a deliberate creator and you direct your thoughts in the direction of your desires. In metaphysics, this is known as a beginner's or learner's consciousness. Here, you are learning to develop an idea of how you want to live or what you want to accomplish in your life, then imagine that goal as already achieved, making it as vivid as possible in your mind's eye and practicing the necessary emotional and mental vibrations to manifest it in your experience. This practice of mental projection and visualization directed at a desired outcome is a miraculous stage in our evolution and it is powerful to discover that we are in control of creating our life experiences. It is exhilarating and liberating to become a conscious creator.

Then, when you progress further in your spiritual development, you understand that in order to manifest your soul purpose, which brings you lasting happiness, satisfaction and fulfillment, you have to use your skills of manifestation not merely to satisfy the physical senses but to live your deeper purpose. Of course, you can still enjoy and appreciate beautiful and luxurious things but joy comes from a deep recognition of the higher power in you, that is expressing Itself in beauty, abundance and splendor all around you, rather than just a gratification of the senses. In this phase of spiritual development, you consciously align with your soul's purpose, which is to love and to express a greater degree of life. In the process, you open yourself up to love, let love fill and become your being and experience directly what the unconditional love of the Divine feels like. As a result, you shift perspective from a material outlook on life toward a spiritual understanding. When you are completely immersed in a feeling of unconditional love, you begin the questioning process. This is the moment and the space in which God's vision for your life, which is the same thing as your soul's purpose, reveals itself to you. When you are in the feeling-space of unconditional divine love, you will experience a deep knowing of what you have to embody or become in order to manifest God's vision for you.

Your soul's expression is constantly changing because with every moment you live you expand and become more. The vantage point from which you act is continuously evolving. But the purpose remains the same, always, and that is to be love and to express a greater degree of life. The answers you receive will differ depending on where you are along the journey but they will always guide you perfectly from the point where you are standing at that very moment into the next step of your development. The process never ends because God's mind is limitless and infinite, and it is eternally expressing. When you align yourself with It, you enter into a spiritual growth process whereby you become an ever expanding space for the divine idea to express through.

Soul purpose visioning is about self-transformation. You learn to raise your vibrations to match those of God. God is divine unconditional love, so you establish the frequency of unconditional love within yourself. In Buddhism, this is called the Bodhisattva's Path. A bodhisattva is an embodiment of unconditional love who wishes to attain enlightenment (the highest form of self-knowledge, or lived Oneness with God) for the sake of all living beings. When your intention springs from unconditional love, you vibrate to the divine frequency, which is also the frequency of your true self, the Christ-consciousness within.

We only have to read the newspapers, watch the news on TV, or listen to office chatter, to realize that the mass consciousness is still in the victim stage of consciousness evolution. At this time, few people have realized the profound truth that they are deliberate creators who have the power to control their own lives with the thoughts they choose to think. Less people still are willing to surrender their personal desires to their soul purpose as specified by Divine Will. Most of humanity is not yet able to experience and align with the Divine Will, because doing so requires a degree of sensitivity to subtle energies and an understanding of the illusion of ego. Aligning with Divine Will is aligning with your true self and your soul's purpose, because your authentic self is the Self that the Divine Will created in an act of self-expression. On a soul level, you are an emanation of the divine, and the Divine Will and your Soul Will, or life purpose, are one. When even a few people align with Divine Will and transform their lives accordingly, the qualities of Divine Will, in other words, Soul Will, or authentic self-expression, can be experienced by many, and ultimately everyone.

The unicorns, eternally conscious of their divine nature, have told me:

"In order to take the next evolutionary step, humanity has to align with, understand, and integrate the energies of Divine Will. The necessary changes for a quantum leap in human consciousness can be brought about by humanity focussing its will collectively as a group -- inspired by love, articulated through the intellect, and under guidance from the Divine Will, expressing Itself in each individual soul."

On a fundamental level we are all interconnected. It only takes a small number of people consciously choosing to live in alignment with the Divine Will for all of humanity to experience a shift in its orientation to the light. At that point, the higher purpose of humanity can be seen and actualized. The British biologist Rupert Sheldrake has described this phenomenon, in which a potential behaviour becomes accessible the more it is enacted by a group, until a critical threshold is reached and it spreads instantaneously to all members, in his theory of Morphic Resonance.

Desire versus Divine Will

This is the difference in orientation between the manifestation stage and the channeling and Being stages; a shift from the material towards the spiritual. Desire originates in and can be viewed as your personal will. Desire works from the earth plane upward. Desires that are spiritual in nature, such as the desire for mystical insight and enlightenment, or the desire to serve humanity, can call Divine Will into your life. Divine Will works from the highest planes downward, transforming every level of your being as you surrender to it. When you surrender to Divine Will, you are surrendering the ego-self or conditioned unreal self to the higher power within, your authentic self. Rather than weakening, debilitating or even annihilating you, the act of surrender frees you to be the Real You. By aligning with Divine Will, you align with your authentic self, which is one with your soul and one with Divine Will.

Your personal desires are usually outflows of the ego and often spring from limited, conditioned beliefs. For example, you may wish for a promotion not because you enjoy your job or are especially good at it but because a colleague you don't get along with was promoted above you. But even when you call Divine Will into your life to assist you in fulfilling a specific personality desire, you will soon find that Divine Will overrides your personal will and desires. Your soul sees more for your life than your personality can ever imagine. Intelligence requires the addition of love to become wisdom.

Your desires will change as your personality wants are transformed by Divine Will, because your personality desires will then be for those things that reflect your soul's purpose and the divine plan for your life. Divine Will simply becomes Your will. Divine Will knows the true You, so when you start to live in alignment with Divine Will you start to live your deepest heart's desires. You start doing what you have always wanted to do, always felt a passion for, always wished you were doing but never thought you could.

The Seven Qualities of Divine Will

To fulfil your soul's purpose, you need to align with the energy or vibration of Divine Will on all levels of your being. You do this by meditating on unconditional love and offering yourself as a vessel through which that love may be expressed in thought, word and action. As you call Divine Will into your life, you fulfil your purpose on earth, reveal your highest potential and are of greater service to humanity.

The Unicorns evolve through service to the divine will. They are embodiments of divine love and are a perfect example of consciousness at the "Being" stage of evolution. They are melded or blended in consciousness with the consciousness of the Divine. They appear on this plane to assist us in our ascension toward unity or God consciousness. They work with the seven frequencies of light, which are the seven colours of the rainbow. The source of all seven rainbow colours is one and the same – white light. In the same way that white light splits up into beautiful shades of colour representing different wave frequencies when seen through a prism, there is one Divine Will that manifests as seven qualities that assist you in different areas of manifesting your soul's purpose and goals.

The First Quality of Divine Will: The Will to Initiate

The first quality of Divine Will is the Will to initiate a new vibration of consciousness; to expand consciousness; to attain spiritual insights, inspiration and revelations; and to initiate the true activity of the soul in accordance with the Divine Plan. The Will to Initiate assists you in experiencing one expansion of consciousness after another, progressing into higher, clearer states of awareness. Each expansion of consciousness opens up new possibilities and potential for your life. It initiates the consciousness that allows you to know yourself as light, energy, and awareness; enabling you to carry out the activities that manifest the Divine plan for your life. The Will to Initiate assists you in a fuller expression of the patterns of wholeness and perfection that already exist within you, waiting to unfold. With the expansion of your consciousness into a union with God consciousness comes a re-orientation of your life so that your thoughts, words and actions express your inner light, your true self, and serve the greater Whole of which you are a part.

The Second Quality of Divine Will: The Will to Unify

The Will to Unify brings unity to all parts of your being – the subconscious, conscious and superconscious aspects of your mind. As you integrate the Will to Unify you become magnetic with the glow of this energy. Your capacity to love expands to include ever increasing numbers of people. You experience your oneness with others; you can sense their soul or inner being and the love that radiates from deep within their true selves. When you experience this soul connection you can see the best in people. You help them to reveal it simply through your awareness of this part of them. With the expansive view of unity consciousness you experience the vision of the whole of which you are a part, flowing outward from the centre of your being to include all life: Nature, humankind, all incarnate and discarnate souls, the elementals and Devas, the Ascended Masters, the Angelic Realms, the Higher Planes – all of existence.

The Third Quality of Divine Will: The Will to Evolve

The Will to Evolve connects you to the world of ideas and unlimited possibilities. It assists you in conceiving new ways to create a life of love and joy. This quality of the Divine Will supports you in manifesting those goals, dreams and lifestyle choices that are the divine plan for your life. This is the Will of the weaver. It assists you in putting all the pieces of the puzzle together to form a whole picture. It inspires the creation of beauty through taking the familiar and arranging it into new and more pleasing patterns; in this way revealing an array of new possibilities.

The Fourth Quality of Divine Will: The Will to Harmonize

The Will to Harmonize helps you to release conflict, and create harmony and unity. This Will harmonizes the initial conflict that occurs when two dissimilar energies at different rates of vibrations make contact. It allows them to come together in harmony, such as the energies of your personality or surface mind and the energies of your inner being or Christ consciousness. The Will to Harmonize assists you in the blending of your consciousness with God-Consciousness, aligning you with the Divine plan for your life. It raises your vibrations or frequencies up to the higher planes of existence and allows your consciousness to expand in every way through identification with them. This aspect of Divine Will can facilitate your being in harmony with the Divine Plan of the Universe, and with the highest vibrations of consciousness; with the Masters, Angels, Unicorns and God, or All-That-Is.

The Fifth Quality of Divine Will: The Will to Act

The Will to Act helps you to take action from clear, focused and concise thoughts. You can call upon this Will, also known as the "Door into the Mind of God", to formulate clear, concise thoughts that are infused with light, charged with intention, and that express divine purpose, divine love, and divine ideas. These are thoughts that carry you toward the unfolding of the Divine blueprint of your life and raise your vibration into a new level of consciousness. Thoughts that are illumined with divine love and divine purpose act as messengers of light, bringing light to the planet, all people, and all of creation.

The Will to Act integrates the three aspects of mind to create a pure channel for the thoughts of the Divine to flow through. The three aspects of mind are your surface mind, also called the ego-mind, ego-self or intellect; your true self, also called inner being, authentic self, Christ consciousness, God consciousness or the divine spark within; and the Unified Field, also called Source, The All, The Absolute, Infinite Intelligence, Divine Mind, Divine Matrix, or God. Your Inner Being or True Self is an individuated expression of the Universal Consciousness. Your surface mind produces all conditioned, imposed thought processes arising from an illusion of separation. In Buddhist philosophy, we have the analogous model of the "root mind" (The Void, The All), the "subtle mind" (the true self) and the "gross mind" (the intellect). In Christian spirituality, we have the Holy Trinity of Father (God), Son (human consciousness or intellect) and Holy Spirit (Christ consciousness, Higher Self or God-mind within). These are all different systems of explaining the same underlying principle.

With the Will to Act, the "three minds unite". When the three minds integrate, your mind fulfils its purpose of being a channel for the pure inflow of higher consciousness energy, allowing your personality to become a clear channel for Divine Will.

The Sixth Quality of Divine Will: The Will to Cause

The Will to Cause helps you to embody your highest ideals. This quality of the Divine Will shifts the motivating impulse of manifestation, actions, thoughts and creative drives from personality desires to the ideals of your true self. When you are living your soul's purpose, all that you do brings you freedom, joy and fulfilment rather than suffering, confusion, or pain. You can work with the Will to Cause to deepen your commitment to living by spiritual principles and thus experience more peace and harmony in your life. You can call upon this Will to sense your soul's goals for your life, and to understand what needs to be created, and what you need to become, in order to express your soul's vision and the Divine blueprint of your life.

The Seventh Quality of Divine Will: The Will to Express

The Will to Express helps you to manifest in a methodical, systematic and organized way the expression of Divine Love in your life. This Will synthesizes consciousness and matter. It assists with the manifestation of perfect forms that express the beauty, love and light of divinity. This quality of Divine Will is also called the Manifesting Ray, the Violet Ray, and the Ray of Ceremonial Order. The words of power for this Will are "The Higher and Lower Meet". It assists you, the Divine Self, in bringing your limitless light, spiritual power, joy, wisdom, and love to the personality self. This aspect of Divine Will assists in creating forms, circumstances, and relationships that express the Divine Self, bringing heaven to earth.

How to Practise Divine Love: Practical Advice from the Unicorns

The unicorns have given me two specific messages on how to express Divine Love in my life. One message is concerned with expressing love within the family, and the other is a message about healing.

Make Divine Love Your Currency

Every family has a currency, let yours be love.

When I received this message, I asked my unicorn guide what other currencies might be in use and received the response: "Guilt, anger, competition, fear, and disconnection."

The Magical Healing Ability of Divine Love and Laughter

Love is the best medicine, but laughter is the next best thing.

After the unicorns had given me this message on the powerful healing potential of laughter, I researched the medical benefits of laughter and found the following:

- **Laughter relaxes the whole body.** A good, hearty laugh relieves physical tension and stress, leaving your muscles relaxed for up to 45 minutes after.
- **Laughter boosts the immune system.** Laughter decreases stress hormones and increases immune cells and infection-fighting antibodies, thus improving your resistance to disease.
- **Laughter triggers the release of endorphins,** the body's natural feel-good chemicals. Endorphins promote an overall sense of well-being and can even temporarily relieve pain.

- **Laughter protects the heart.** Laughter improves the function of blood vessels and increases blood flow, which can help protect you against a heart attack and other cardiovascular problems.[15]

I remember the day of the unicorn workshop with Flavia-Kate as one of the most laughter-filled of my life. There was a happy, joyful, mirthful energy in the group and we all felt as if we had known each other for a long time, although most of us were meeting for the first time. The laughter was another form of healing that the unicorns were sending that day.

CHAPTER 6

Prosperity with the Unicorns

"Gratitude is not only the greatest of virtues but the parent of all the others."
- Cicero

What is Prosperity?

Prosperity is a state of mind which is characterized by a feeling of joy and peace within and about you. True prosperity is not only about financial wealth, but includes areas such as love, health and happiness. Having one of these things without the other is not true prosperity, according to metaphysical understanding. If you feel impoverished in one area of your life, such as love, for example, this feeling of poverty, loss or lack will affect other areas of your mind in which thinking about other things, such as finances, or health, takes place, thus diminishing your feeling of "wealth" or abundance in all areas of your consciousness.

The unicorns teach that the right mental attitude for attracting true prosperity is a state of faith, or continual expectancy, a state of mind that is always open to inspiration from the Higher Self within you. Your Higher Self is the Ultimate Mind, or God-Consciousness, part of you. Your authentic self is an inlet and an outlet of Divine Mind. This means that you receive inspiration from your Higher Self or God-Mind and express these ideas in outward manifestation.

You use the Mind of God every time you think. God, or Universal Mind, expresses Itself in you, through you and as you.

The unicorns help you attune to the wisdom of your higher mind, which always knows that God, as the Manifesting Universe, is the only true Source of supply and prosperity. In meditation, you realize and experience, directly, the inner presence of your true self. Knowing, on a soul level, that God is truly within you, at the central core of your Being and consciousness-mind-intelligence, produces the greatest mental attitude for achieving prosperity.

Unicorn Prosperity Meditation

The unicorns have given me the following prosperity practice. It is very affective for aligning with the God-Mind and tuning into the true source of all abundance and prosperity within your own mind. The unicorns want you to know that they love you unconditionally and want to see you living the life that makes your heart sing, the life you came here to live. They wish to remind you of your true nature and your soul's purpose, offering unconditional love and inspiring the best in you. They share instructions on the true prosperity consciousness to help you fully express your higher self in the physical world.

Enter into a state of relaxation and meditation, and then affirm the following, while feeling the truth of the affirmation in every cell of your being. When you feel a great upwelling of gratitude, joy, or peace, you will know that your affirmation has been successful in connecting you with the Divine Mind. Repeat this affirmation and meditation every day, and especially whenever you feel anxious, worried or frustrated about the flow of abundance in your life.

My mind is God's mind. I use the mind of God each time I think and as God always succeeds, I must always succeed. I have the wisdom, intelligence and creative power of the entire universe working in me and through me, as I attain and attract prosperity. In this state of soul, I am confident, knowing that the "mystical magic" of God is working in me, for my prosperity, each and every day.

Prosperity Is Always Available to You

The unicorns are examples of souls, or individuated streams of consciousness, in perfect union with God. They always act from their Higher Self, the Divine Spark within, because they are never separated from the Mind of God. There is an easy way to discover to what degree you are living life from your authentic self. Look at your life. A sense of separation from God shows up in your life as the absence of your desires, as the absence of joy, love and creative fulfillment. It is important to remember that many of the things in your life that you perceive as "negative" or "bad" experiences are in fact this sense of separation. In other words, the experience of separation manifests in your life as the absence of your abundance, rather than its presence. But is it really absent? No, of course not, because you can never be outside of God, therefore the Abundance of God is always available to you. However, when you exert your free will to turn away from the experience of prosperity, shutting down the avenues through which it can reach you, and seeing and expecting only the negative -- then poverty, negativity and lack are the only things you allow yourself to experience.

A Grateful Mind is a Powerful Wealth Magnet

Lao Tzu, the Chinese philosopher and founder of Taoism, said:
"If you look to others for fulfillment, you will never truly be fulfilled. If your happiness depends on money, you will never be happy with yourself. Be content with what you have. Rejoice in the way things are. When you realize there is nothing lacking, the whole world belongs to you."[16]

What this means is that gratitude, rejoicing in the way things are, is true wealth. We can never experience true wealth and abundance unless we cultivate a mind of gratitude. Even if you have millions in the bank, unless you have a mind of gratitude and abundance, you will still *feel* poor. When you have a poverty consciousness, it does not matter how much you accumulate, you always feel that you don't have enough and you are constantly afraid of losing what you do have.

Jesus said, "Perfect love casts out fear." (1 John 4:18) The 13th century Persian Sufi mystic and poet Rumi wrote, "I merge with my Beloved, when I participate in love".[17] Perfect love is the result of your continual union with God as your Beloved in loving reciprocation. Giving and receiving is the principle of prosperity. Without giving there can be no receiving and without receiving there can be no giving. Jesus clearly articulated this divine law: "Give, and it will be given to you." (Luke 6:38) Giving and receiving are two sides of the same coin, as they are happening simultaneously as a divine dance between lover and Beloved, between God and you.

Gratitude affirms abundance, whereas worry affirms lack. Many people win the lottery and lose all the money within a short space of time. You need to practice the correct mental attitude toward prosperity. Unless you do, it will always elude you. Prosperity is first and foremost a *feeling*. Unless you can get yourself into the feeling-space of prosperity, you can never truly experience it because you are not in vibrational alignment with it. Worry, doubt, and fear are all signs of a consciousness of lack, or poverty. The Mind of God is all abundant, all-resourceful, and all-inclusive. There is no lack in the Mind of God. It simply does not exist. A perception of lack is always a sign of disconnection from God. Joseph Murphy, in *The Power of Your Subconscious Mind*, writes, "Poverty is a mental illness",[18] meaning it is a mental delusion, a mistaken perception that is focused on lack, which is really the absence of God (abundance).

Money is not the root of all evil. The actual quote from the Bible reads, "For *the love* of money is the root of all evil: which while some coveted after, they have erred from the faith, and pierced themselves through with many sorrows" (1 Timothy 6:10 KJV). Money is a symbol of energy. It is a method of exchange. There is nothing evil about money itself. What this Bible passage warns you about is making the acquisition of money the sole goal, aim and purpose of your life. The same applies to the much-quoted passage: "It is easier for a camel to go through the eye of a needle, than for a rich man to enter into the kingdom of God." (Matthew 19:24) The metaphysical meaning of this statement is that a purely material focus and the acquisition of riches for their own sake will make it impossible for you to know the "kingdom of God", which is the God-Mind within. This concept is explained again, very clearly by Jesus in the Bible passage that says, "Then give to Caesar what is Caesar's, and to God what is God's". (Luke 20:25) In other words, in all your transactions remain firmly rooted in the idea of money as limitless God-substance. You purchase an item in a shop, and you hand the cashier your money (material plane, "give to Caesar what is Caesar's"), but as you do this, you are conscious that you are a channel for the limitless flow of prospering substance (spiritual plane, "to God what is God's"). This is a mental practice that will help you immeasurably in forming and maintaining a prosperity consciousness.

Money will not make you happy. Poverty will not make you happy. Happiness is a feeling. To many people, money represents security, independence and freedom of expression. Money is a way to bless people and things; to give energy and power to causes, people or products you believe in. All these things are ultimately *feelings* — of gratitude, abundance, love, joy, freedom.

In other words, what attracts prosperity to you is not hard work, supreme effort, or extreme competitiveness. These practices may lead to an accumulation of money, or they may not, but the joy and freedom of true prosperity will elude you unless you think yourself into alignment with it. The fastest way to achieve alignment with the vibration of abundance is to practice gratitude. The universe loves a grateful person. As you find more and more things in your life to be thankful for, life will present you with more and more things to be thankful for. It is the Law of Attraction at work, and it never fails.

The practice of gratitude is a quick path to the Mind of God. Gratitude is an expression of love, of appreciation, of joy. God loves, appreciates and blesses every atom of the universe. When we do the same, we are in perfect harmony with the Mind of God. When this happens, we are able to experience true abundance and prosperity. You see why the practice of gratitude is so important to true prosperity consciousness? Without gratitude, you disconnect yourself from the Source of all abundance, the Mind of God. The great 13th century mystic Meister Eckhart said, "If the only prayer you say in your whole life is *thank you*, that would suffice."

Think Big, Feel Go(o)d

All you need to realize to begin your journey into wealth consciousness is that you have already arrived. Since you are created in the image and likeness of God, the moment you were thought into being as an individualized expression of God, "all that the Father hath" (John 16:15) became your divine inheritance. Abundance is your natural state. It is not something you acquire, or get. It is something you are, something you tune into. In the absence of all limiting, negative thoughts you are perfectly happy, and fully abundant.

The greatest discovery of all time is to become aware of the power of God, and the union of your own mind with the Mind of God. Coming into alignment with your authentic self helps you to become aware of the rich potentialities within you. The Bible says, "Acquaint now thyself with Him and be at peace, and therefore good shall come unto thee". (Job 22:21) The only thing that truly matters is to tune into the higher self, or God-Mind within you. Remember, you go where your vision is. If you hold subconscious beliefs of lack or failure, you may work very hard 16 hours a day and still, success will elude you. If your premise is false, the result will be false as well. Before engaging in any action, establish the correct premise in the knowledge that the mind is syllogistic in its functioning and that it works infallibly from premise to conclusion. Act from your authentic self. Think with your God-Mind. Think big, feel big, and know in your heart that you are now working together with God, the cosmic power that creates worlds.

You are a spiritual being, living in a spiritual universe, conducted by a perfect God, operating under His perfect Divine law. When you realize this, you will never feel inadequate or inferior; and you will not be critical or judgemental of others either. We see within others that which we perceive in ourselves. As you align with God, you will stop projecting your feelings of inadequacy, shortcoming, or inferiority onto others. When you live from your Higher Self, you radiate confidence, joy, and a healing vibration that blesses everything and everyone you come into contact with.

When you start to feel anxious or doubtful about the manifestation of something you are waiting for, hand it over to God with the words: *"I accept this, God, or in Your wisdom something grander, greater, and more wonderful that I cannot imagine as of yet. Thank you."*

Affirmative Prayer for Prosperity

The following is an affirmation or prayer the unicorns have taught me for the cultivation of Prosperity Consciousness:

"God is everything, everywhere, and everyone. I am an expression of God. My mind and God's Mind are one. I reflect Divine Intelligence and Divine Wisdom at all times. My brain is a symbol of my capacity to think wisely and spiritually. God's ideas unfold within my mind in perfect sequence. I know that the inner desires of my heart come from God within me. God's will for me is life, love, joy, truth, abundance and beauty. My dreams for my life are God's dreams for me. The Still Small Voice whispers into my ear revealing to me my perfect answer. I refuse to accept the limited and conditioned voice of the ego-mind intellect as truth. Turning within, I sense and feel the rhythm of the Divine. I hear the melody of God whispering its message of love to me. I am always confident, balanced, serene, and calm, because I know that God will always reveal to me the perfect solution to all my needs. I feel deep gratitude for God's eternal love, guidance and givingness. I give all glory to God. And So It Is."

Affirmative prayer, also called spiritual mind treatment because it "treats" or directs the mind to recognize its true nature and to manifest that which is desired, is based on the understanding that we will naturally, lawfully, create what we hold in our thoughts. To affirm means to state positively, while prayer is speaking to God. By employing affirmative prayer, we use positive statements of Truth and thanksgiving to speak to God. Jesus of Nazareth, the Buddha, and all self-realized minds realized their communion with God and for this reason, they used affirmative prayer in their communications with Divinity. Jesus guided us in the use of affirmative prayer when he said, "So I tell you, whatever you ask for in prayer, believe that you have received it, and it will be yours". (Mark 11:24) Affirmative prayer uses the spiritual laws of this Universe to unfold and manifest the experience you desire in your life. The universal laws can be summed up as: *It is done unto you as you believe.*

Any form of prayer that begs, beseeches, haggles, bribes or otherwise tries to convince God to grant whatever is needed or desired is an ineffective way of praying because it assumes lack and is based on doubt. Whatever you desire has already been granted by God. *The universe always says yes.* But in order to receive it, you have to allow it in. The way to allow it in is to align yourself with its vibration. If you pray, *"I don't have enough money. Why do I never have enough money? I can't afford to pay my bills! Please, God, please send me some money now!"*, you are praying from a perspective of lack. When you state, *"I can't afford to pay my bills!"*, the universe responds with *"Yes, you can't afford to pay your bills!"* and the financial abundance you seek cannot manifest in your experience. Where have you gone wrong? You think you have made it clear that you want a greater inflow of money but in fact, you have not affirmed what you want, you have merely stated what you lack and so the universe, faithfully and logically, brings more lack into your experience. When you are looking towards darkness, you cannot perceive light. It defies all logic. When you shift your focus to affirming your wishes and desires, you believe, trust and *know* that they are being fulfilled. You are now affirming the fulfilment of your wishes, and by this shift, you are now filled with hope, expectation and gratitude for the perfect, logical workings of the laws of the universe that deliver to you what you want. You know how to utilize and the laws and you are now expecting greatness. In this way, you are aligning yourself with the vibration of what you *do* want. It can now freely and abundantly come to you because you are allowing it in.

5 Easy Steps to Prayer that Works

Affirmative prayer is based on five steps: Recognition, Unification, Realization, Thanksgiving, and Release. "Be anxious for nothing;

but in every thing by prayer and supplication with thanksgiving let your requests be made known unto God." (Philippians 4:6 NKJV)

To begin your affirmative prayer, state the purpose for the prayer treatment. In essence, you are "treating" or thinking your mind into alignment with God. First state the condition you desire to change. Then state the changed condition you expect to experience. Affirm that it is already given, manifest and complete.

Desire: "I want to experience more loving and harmonious relationships in my life."

Affirmation: "I am now experiencing relationships that are fulfilling, genuine, inspiring, harmonious and fun."

Then begin the treatment as follows:

Step 1: Recognition. The first step involves the recognition that God, Universal Consciousness, Divine Mind, First Cause, The All, The Absolute, Source or whatever term you prefer is omnipresent, omnipotent, and omniscient. In other words, God is all-inclusive, all-powerful, and all-knowing. The One Mind of God is everywhere and everything, at all times, and nothing exists outside of God.

Step 2: Unification. The second step is realizing that you are One with the Allness of God. You are an individuated expression of the one Universal Consciousness. God is present in you as your Higher Self, Divine Spark or God-Mind. You are a thought in the Mind of God and any thought you think is also thought by the Universal Mind of God.

Step 3 Realization. This is where you state your desire in the affirmative. It has happened, it is granted, and it is already complete in the Mind of God. Since God is flowing through everything, God is present in you. Any thought you think is also thought in the Mind of God. All the riches of the Universe are your heritage because of who-you-are, an emanation of God. You only have to realize the truth that you are one with whatever good you are asking for. In that knowledge it will manifest in your life for the highest good.

Step 4 Thanksgiving. This is one of the most important steps. A feeling of gratitude and thanksgiving is essential to spiritual manifestation. Generate a deep sense of gratitude for the Goodness of God as your life and the good that is taking form in your experience. Have faith that it is so and express this faith through gratitude.

Step 5 Release. Release your desires, wishes and dreams to the Universal Mind of God or what physicists call the Unified Field of First Cause knowing that all that you have asked for that is good will manifest. You have planted the seeds and they will manifest according the Universal Law of Cause and Effect because "as ye sow, so shall ye reap". It is done. And So It Is.[4]

Prosperity and Poverty are States of Mind

In Chinese, *Tint To* means the "Universal Law of Abundance", by which you can be all that you can be, because you are of the Tao, and the Tao is all-abundant. This Universal Law simply tells you that, as you are of this spiritual energy of the Tao, so you are all-abundant.[19] Prosperity is a state of mind, an attitude, a deep sense of knowing that God is our eternal, opulent, and constant Source and supply. It is an inner feeling of peace, security, joy and omnipotence. Poverty is also a state of mind, but instead of faith in the eternal abundance of God you are placing your faith in your fears of lack and limitation. You either have faith in God or faith in your fears. Whichever faith you choose will determine what you experience and manifest. The key to living abundantly and claiming your divine heritage as a child of God is shifting your core belief from "I don't have enough" to "I always have enough".

We are all equal parts of God. Contrary to outer appearances, we are all equally abundant and prosperous but not everyone is laying claim to their divine inheritance. The rich get rich, and the poor get poorer, "For whosoever hath, to him shall be given, and he shall have more abundance: but whosoever hath not, from him shall be taken away even that he hath" (Matthew 13:12 KJV), is a Truth

---

4   Perhaps the most frequently used and well-known affirmation is the word "Amen", which is of Hebrew origin and can be translated as "so be it" or "and so it is", affirming the truth of whatever was written or said immediately before.

that does not seem to be fair according to worldly logic, as we feel that the poor should also be able prosper.

In reality, nobody is lacking anything except for the knowledge of who-we-really-are and what is available to us. All human problems, including poverty, originate in this lack of understanding. This is why *A Course In Miracles* teaches that a sense of separation from God is the only lack we ever truly have to heal. It reminds us that Separation is a dream from which we need to awaken. Awakening, which is also called liberation or salvation occurs when we hear the Holy Spirit, the call to awaken, in ourselves and in others, thereby accepting our oneness with the other that removes the sense of separation which gave rise to the dream in the beginning. Using the gifts, talents and skills you have for the higher purpose of serving God by being the instrument through which Divine Love is expressed in the world, and increasing the well-being and happiness of others, ensures that all your dreams will come true and all your needs will be met. If you are a talented cook, you can make others happy by serving delicious, creative dishes which honour God's creation and promote the happiness and good health of your guests. If you are a talented designer, you can use your skills to create objects of beauty, to lift people's spirits and celebrate the bounty of God's handiwork. If you are a talented singer, you can write and perform songs that celebrate joy, life, and love -- helping people feel the thrill of being alive and bringing them in touch with the rhythm of the cosmos. Any skill, talent or gift you have is there for a reason. The best way to use what you have been given, and certainly the way to true prosperity, is to celebrate life, embody love, and glorify God.

Connect with the Universal Source and let Itself channel through you. Begin to move into the consciousness that is prosperous: prosperous in love, in ideas, in expressions, in everything that you dream of doing. Feel that you live in that consciousness of prosperity. It belongs to you. When you feel prosperous you are in tune with the Universe and its unlimited resources, creativity and power.

The unicorns teach that on a fundamental level prosperity *is* *spirituality.* God said, "Thou art ever with me and all that I have is thine." (Luke 15:31 KJV) The unicorns advise us: *"Begin now to talk plenty, think plenty, and give thanks for plenty. Enlist all the members of your household in the same work. Make it a game. It is a lot of fun, and even better, it actually works."*

Exercise: Write a New Story

What does this imply on a practical level? What can you do right now to start manifesting your desires in accordance with the laws of the universe? The one action you can take today is to tell a new story. Put your dreams, hopes and visions into words and on paper. Your vision for your life may seem unrealistic and you may have no idea how to accomplish it, as I did with this book for example. The task may seem unattainable, insurmountable even. This is not the time to fret over the "how", focus on the "what" instead. Allow yourself to visualize yourself living your dream life. What are you doing? Where are you living? Who is with you? What are you tasting, seeing, smelling, hearing, touching? How are you feeling? Engage all your senses in this exercise. Allow yourself to dream and let go of all resistance. The universe has access to many more ways to manifest this vision and enable the Real You to shine than your mind can imagine. The old story of who-you-are may have included much resistance in the form of "I can't", "I mustn't", "I shouldn't", "I have to be sensible about this", "I don't see why this should happen to me", "I am not good enough", "I don't deserve this", "Things always end up going wrong for me", "just when I think things are improving, I get knocked down again", "it's better if I don't even try, that way I can't be disappointed" and many more excuses we find not to live our life's purpose and feel happy and fulfilled. Be honest with yourself. Any time you find yourself thinking a limiting, resisting thought, your higher self does not agree with your projection and as a result, you feel a vibrational discord which expresses itself as guilt, shame, lack of self-esteem, fear and pain. Replace this thought with a thought that feels better to you. Instead of affirming "this always happens to me", write a new story and begin to resolve this pattern by saying "I like knowing that I can improve this situation and change my feeling about it just by thinking different thoughts".

Faith is really your consent to let your own uniqueness unfold and to let that which is attracted by your uniqueness manifest in your life. When Jesus said, "all things are possible to them that believe", he did not mean that a sparrow can become an eagle or that a non-sporty person can win the Olympics. You cannot become something that is not the outer demonstration of your inner potential. You can only *be* you. But you can reveal and express more of the You that may have been frustrated for a long time. Of course, you can use the manifestation process to create "second hand" experiences, things you believe you want because others have them, aiming "to become like him" or "have what she has". But when you achieve something that is not an outward expression of your own uniqueness, then you may lose even when you win. Like the "rejection syndrome" complication in transplant surgery, things that do not come from your own soul pattern will not "stick". They will disintegrate and not bring you lasting happiness. When you construct your life's vision on another's ideas, you build on sand. When you look to the God-Mind within for the vision, you build on rock. The important thing is to know yourself. Be true to yourself. Have faith in the cosmic process that will unfold in you like the life force unfolds in the lily of the field. "Consider the lilies how they grow: they toil not, they spin not; and yet I say unto you, that Solomon in all his glory was not arrayed like one of these". (Luke 12:27 KJV)

Ask and Ye Shall Receive

There is no idea of lack anywhere in the Divine Mind. The Divine Mind is perfectly abundant, endlessly creative and has limitless resources. Just as you do not use up your neighbour's supply of air by breathing because there is plenty of supply for all, so do you also not use up your neighbour's financial supply by the money you manifest into your experience. There is an endless supply of substance in the universe to mould into any experience, demonstration or supply you choose. If the mind can see it and believe it, it can create it. *"Ask, and it shall be given you; seek, and ye shall find; knock, and it shall be opened unto you: For every one that asketh receiveth; and he that seeketh findeth; and to him that knocketh it shall be opened."* (Matthew 7:7-8 KJV)

The Bible is very clear in describing the neverending flow of substance and abundance from the Creator into His Creation. It also provides us with an easy-to-follow manual for spiritual manifestation, warning us of the pitfalls of seeking financial and material wealth merely for its own sake and ignoring the broader, spiritual dimension of life. Finally, it teaches us that in order to consciously manifest, we have to release old patterns of fear (mistaken thoughts) and feel that we *deserve* to receive. In other words, we have to ask (decide what we want) and allow (feel that we deserve to receive and expect goodness). *"Ye have not, because ye ask not." (James 4:2 KJV)*

You are a spiritual being having a physical experience and when you forget that, you are out of alignment with who-you-really-are. The flawed premise yields flawed results. The Beloved has abundantly provided for each part of Itself. Our unique gifts, talents and skills are the means we have been given through which to manifest prosperity in our life; by enriching others' lives, living our heart's desire and glorifying God. *"And whatsoever ye shall ask in my name, that will I do, that the Father may be glorified in the Son. If ye shall ask any thing in my name, I will do it." (Matthew 7:7-8 KJV)*

The unicorns say: *"Abundance is your birthright. Claim it and glorify the Life of God!"*

CHAPTER 7

Unicorn Dreams, Signs and Symbols

"Dreams pass into the reality of action. From the actions stems the dream again; and this interdependence produces the highest form of living."
- Anaïs Nin

Unicorn Dreams

Ever since my unicorn self-attunement during meditation I have been experiencing frequent unicorn dreams. They are always blissful, joyous and inspiring. Often I dream that I am flying on my unicorn's back across the sky. Stars shoot from its horn, blessing everything in the area where they touch the ground. In my dreams, I see webs of golden light spreading where the unicorn energy has descended.

In my meditations, I often replicate this scenario and visualize unicorn blessings cascading down on impoverished areas and areas of darkness, violence, greed and hostility. The unicorns have only one mission: They emanate, foster and spread pure divine love and assist us in awakening to our true nature and unity consciousness. The angelic realms are overjoyed when lightworkers join their mission and assist them in being a light in the world.

A person with a high energy frequency, who has a vision beyond their own surface self and who, from a feeling of interconnectedness, wishes to help others and raise the collective consciousness of humankind in the process, sends out a bright light which is visible to the angels and unicorns. Such a lightworker is easily identifiable to the light beings of the higher realms because of their high vibration which distinguishes them from their surroundings. Even if a single lightworker lives in an area of deprivation, squalor or violence, the vibration of the whole area will be lifted as a result. The image that the unicorns have when flying over such an area is one of darkness. In the blackness, the lightworker is easily spotted because they appear as a column of white light shooting skyward like the beam of a very bright flashlight. You can also picture it like a thick dark fog which is pierced by the luminous light of a fog light, illuminating all that surrounds it.

In dream work and dream interpretation, dreaming of unicorns is seen as a very positive sign. Unicorn dreams are associated with purity, magical consciousness, and union of the divine and animal (physical) nature. Dream analysts believe that when you dream of unicorns, it is a subconscious message to ask yourself: *Where in my life am I ready to align my physical nature with my spiritual nature?*[20]

In my experience, when you dream of unicorns, you are meeting them on the inner planes. This means that they are already working with you. When unicorns appear to you, whether in meditation or in your dreams, they are giving you healing and also recruiting you to join them in their mission of raising the consciousness of humankind, one person at a time. Unicorns are here to show us that the true meaning of life is to express divine love in our own unique way.

When a unicorn accepts you onto his or her back, this is an invitation to experience the true freedom, faith and love that comes with being in connection with Source energy. Unicorns are free and can never be bridled or saddled but out of generosity and love they may let the spirits of humans and elementals ride on their backs. Such an invitation is an immense honour and should never be taken for granted. Riding on your unicorn's back, travelling the world or crossing the sky, is an exhilarating experience of pure joy, love and abandonment.

We are spiritual beings in a physical body so we all experience a physical life during the day when we are awake and a spiritual life at night when we are asleep. In our dreams, we visit other planets, star systems or dimensions, reconnect with souls that are incarnated in other worlds or are presently in non-physical form. Those of us who are spiritually ready, attend spiritual "classes" given by the angels and other spiritual guides. Many of us are unaware of the spiritual work we do while asleep, such as helping, rescuing and guiding others, so when we wake up exhausted after seven or eight hours of sleep we wonder why we are so tired when we have just slept for many hours. It is a scientific fact that the human brain never rests (there is always brain wave activity, even in the deepest stages of sleep) and in fact, a night's dream work can often be more demanding and tiring than our daily tasks and activities.

Unicorn Numbers

Like angels, the unicorns use numbers and numerology to communicate messages to us. When you dream of two unicorns, for example, this can mean that you are coming into balance in one area of your life or that a soul mate is coming into your experience. Two is a number of balance, of sharing and togetherness.

The following is a short list of the significance of the numbers one to nine as they are used by the unicorns to communicate certain messages to you.

Zero – Zero is a cipher, which is the mathematical symbol **0** indicating absence of quantity. Strictly speaking, it is not a number. Zero represents the unmanifest, the unlimited, the eternal. The great mathematician and metaphysician Pythagoras saw Zero as perfection; the Monad, the originator and container of All. The uterus is an ellipse, as is the egg. Zero represents the potentiality, or the origin, of life. As an ellipse the two sides represent ascent and descent, evolution and involution. Zero is a powerful symbol which represents transformation, regeneration and change, sometimes occurring on a profound level.

One: One primarily deals with strong will, positivity, and pure energy. The number one is the number of new beginnings, action and leadership. Symbolically, one represents both kinds of action: physical and mental. When one is recurring in your life, it indicates a time to take action, be optimistic, and initiate change. Frequent sightings of the number one encourage you that your actions will be rewarded.

Two: The symbolic meaning of the number two is kindness, balance, tact, equalization, and duality. It is the number of compromise, cooperation, diplomacy and meditation. The number two represents a quiet power of judgment. Two asks you to transcend your indecision and make a choice. The spiritual meaning of the number two also deals with partnerships and communication. Two calls you to unite with like minds and like ideals. Two reminds you to connect with your authentic self and follow the natural flow of inspiration to live your soul's purpose.

Three: Three represents magic, intuition and productivity. The number three is associated with expression, versatility, and the pure joy of creativity. Three is also a marker of time as it represents past, present and future. Consecutive threes in your life may indicate a need to express yourself creatively, or to reflect on your life's direction in relation to past events and future goals. Three may also represent promising new adventures and assurance of cooperation from others to help with the accomplishment of your goals. Three typically symbolizes reward and success.

Four: Four represents stability, order and foundation. Think of the four seasons, the four directions, the four elements, or the four noble truths in Buddhism. Four symbolizes solidity, calmness, and home. A recurrence of the number four in your life may signify the need to get back to your roots, centre yourself, or take stock of your life. Four also indicates a need for discipline, persistence and endurance, which will pay off in the end.

Five: Five is the number of change, of opportunity, chance and adventure. On the flipside, five also signifies instability, unpredictability and radical changes. On a spiritual level, five draws our attention to the magnificence of life and reminds us to appreciate the powerful flow of energy in and about us. Five has wild vibrations: freedom, enthusiasm and change. When five continues to pop up in your life, be prepared for action, change, and adventure. Get ready for a trip. Remember, trips are not all necessarily taken physically. Some of the most exciting journeys are taken in the inner worlds.

Six: Six represents harmony, balance, sincerity, love, and truth. It is connected to the planet Venus and represents all forms of love relationships: romantic love, motherly love and platonic love. The number six stands for solutions unfolding in a harmonious manner. It guides you towards diplomacy when dealing with sensitive matters. Six reminds you to practise compassion and consciously choose forgiveness in a situation. Pearls and diamonds are associated with the number six. Spiritually, the number six refers to enlightenment; specifically "lighting" your path in areas where you require spiritual and mental balance.

Seven: Seven is the number of analysis and critique. Seven, like three, is associated with magical powers. It is connected with the esoteric, scholarly aspects of magic and is representative of introspection, solitude and a continuous pursuit of the knowledge of universal truths. Seven is concerned with the activation of imagination and manifesting results in our lives through the use of conscious thought and awareness.

Eight: Eight is associated with business, success, wealth, leadership and effective organization. This is due to the fact that the number eight represents continuation, repetition, and cycles. The mathematical symbol for infinity is an 8 turned sideways because the figure has no beginning and no end. Matters of business and wealth largely depend on cycles to achieve their successful manifestation. Prosperity and manifestation work according to the snowball principle: As it continues to roll, in gets bigger and bigger with each turn (cycle). Eight represents this type of powerful momentum.

Nine: Nine brings us to the highest vibrational frequencies in this number sequence. Nine represents attainment, satisfaction, and accomplishment. When you see the number nine, you are being called to recognize your own internal qualities, and use your abilities, skills and talents to make a positive difference in the world.

The Master Numbers

Master Numbers energetically accentuate the meanings of single digits. They are considered to be some of the most powerful vibrations in the universe. They symbolize raw untapped potential and assist you in achieving union consciousness.

When you receive numerical messages, whether Master Numbers (all the same numbers) or Personal Codes (seeing the same mixed numbers over and over again), stop for one full minute, allowing this energy to be birthed through you. Focus on your deepest desire and see it as reality. The universe has just taken a picture of your thoughts. Empty yourself of any preconceived notions and let the light from your unicorn's horn smooth out any creases in your intentions. Each and every number message within your personal experience is triggering your subconscious into a new pattern of being.

00, 000, or 0000

The Great Void. The Cosmic Egg. The Universal Womb. The unknown What Is To Be, that has not been birthed yet. The portal of creation before creation. This is known under many names: First cause, The Unmanifest, Breath of God, Unified Field, Source, Space, Consciousness, Limitless, Unknowable, Truth, Love, The All, Alpha and Omega, God. 0 is a reminder that you are always One with the primordial power of the universe. Feel yourself within the centre of the 0 embraced by the Creator as you are held and loved unconditionally like a foetus enveloped in the utero. Meander around the inner circle of self, completing what needs to be completed.

11, 111, or 11:11

You are reminded to let go of conditioned and limited ego-mind beliefs and come into alignment with your authentic self. Watch your thoughts. You are a conscious creator. You are becoming One with the Oversoul in the abundant creation of your heart's desires.

22, 222, or 22:22

Keep holding your vision and intent, knowing that what you have planted through your words, thoughts and actions will grow and bear fruit in accordance with the universal laws. This is the number of Genius and Inspiration. Risk being an Idealist; a Visionary. You are a leader; a bridge builder. Compassion, service and philanthropy lead to universal transformation.

33,333 or 3333

You are connecting with highly evolved spiritual beings, ascended masters, angels, and unicorns. The trinity is the holiness within all of your choices. Your body, mind, and spirit are in agreement with your soul's evolution. This number reminds you of the importance of your connection with the wisdom of the Oversoul and seeing the sacredness in all of your choices, no matter what the outcome.

44, 444 or 4444

New opportunity is coming your way. Build your future steadily -- thought by thought, step by step. Do not allow the sceptics, naysayers and doubters to flatten your dreams with their negativity. Believe deeply, hold firm to the vision, until you see the proof. Hold on through all choices and changes. Stay balanced in what you know to be divine truth and your power of manifestation will increase. Build your house (life) on a solid foundation (spiritual truth), not on sand (material awareness).

"*Therefore everyone who hears these words of mine and puts them into practice is like a wise man who built his house on the rock. But everyone who hears these words of mine and does not put them into practice is like a foolish man who built his house on sand.*" (Matthew 7: 24, 26)

55, 555 or 5555

You are being "nudged" toward whole-brain thinking. Develop an integral consciousness through meditation and contemplation. You are a Way shower; a leader to the light; a universal mediator. Through awakening to ultimate oneness you achieve ultimate freedom. Mental telepathy and clairvoyance are the result of the integrated awareness of universal consciousness.

66, 666 or 6666

Seeing the 6, which is the number of love and truth, multiplied, is a very positive sign. You are actualizing cosmic consciousness, achieving initiation into the inner mysteries through meditation, transforming (material) passion into (spiritual) compassion. You are activating *kundalini* life force energy, transmuting old and worn conditioned beliefs which no longer serve you into the more expanded, broader perspective of your authentic self. In this way, by finding the kingdom of God within, you are becoming a holistic human; a peacemaker; a light in the world. This leads to Divine fulfilment. You are living your soul's purpose.

77, 777 or 7777

You are a spiritual being having a human experience. The body is the temple of the soul. You have temporarily clothed yourself in this physical form. It is time for introspection. Turn away from the external world and towards Spirit. Sevens bring you home to the place where miracles are a commonplace event, where you can fly and dance in the stars in any form you choose. Seven is a place where wonder, magic and miracles are seen as natural happenings. Seven is your natural state of being. You are in conscious union with universal intelligence or God.

88, 888 or 8888

The multiple 8 symbolizes a portal to infinity ushering you past all previous limitations. Transcend your everyday beliefs about reality and your constraints within it. Fly to the moon and stop by the Milky Way on your way back. Multiple eights signalize accomplishment, prosperity and business success with a bonus gift of universal blessings. You are finally remembering your divine inheritance promised to you by your Creator. Turn your back on earthly limitation and walk bravely forward and upward into a place of opulence, riches and bounty.

99, 999 or 9999

You are entering the next level of Love: of heart, of soul and service to the planetary evolution through healing of the Self. Entry and exits all take place in the same breath. A quantum leap into unknown worlds comes through the nine. Are you ready to see and be more than you are in this moment in time?

The next time you see 11:11 on the clock, stop and feel the subtle energies around you. The 11:11 is a wake-up call you sent to yourself; a reminder of your true purpose here on Earth. Usually during times of heightened energy or accelerated personal change you will notice multiple numbers more frequently. These number messages belong to the Greater Reality which is the reality that is based on Oneness rather than duality. When you notice them in your life, you are tuning into this Greater Reality and opening yourself up to receiving messages and guidance from your higher self and the beings of higher consciousness, such as the unicorns and angels. (While writing this paragraph the digits on my computer clock read 22:11!)

Number sequences, for example 111 or 11:11 on the clock, mean that the energy around this number is very strong in your life right now. In this example, you are being nudged (not too subtly!) to keep your thoughts positive and focussed on your goals because it is time to initiate productive change in your life. It is also a sign that you are open to receiving guidance and are on the right track.

Maybe you have had experiences like me, where you find your thoughts or conversations "monitored", approved and enjoyed by the unicorns and other higher dimensional beings. For example, a few weeks ago I was in my kitchen talking about the year 2012 and the collective evolution of human consciousness toward a recognition of our essential unity with universal intelligence. When I looked up I noticed that the time on the oven clock was reading 20:12. I was blown away. It seemed so unlikely and such a strange coincidence. But then, being a firm believer in the idea that there are no coincidences, only synchronicities, I deduced that the unicorns had been listening in on my explanations and were using my oven clock to communicate their message of approval to me. On another occasion, in the process of writing this book, when I saved a draft of the manuscript, the word number count totalled up to 26,266 – the unicorns love the number six as it represents their energies of harmony, spiritual evolution and divine love. The number two relates to living one's life purpose, and joyful manifestation, so I take this number as a message from the unicorns signalling to me that they are happy with the book content and that I am on course, following the path of my life's purpose, expressing divine love and sharing spiritual truth, by writing it.

Unicorn Signs and Symbols

The unicorns take supreme pleasure in communicating with humans who are ready to connect with their energy and are able to help them in their mission of raising the collective consciousness of humankind. When unicorns help us, sometimes they do so in ways which we do not immediately recognize as spiritual guidance. They often deliver answers, nudges, messages, and warnings through signs and symbols, or attention-grabbing occurrences in your life, which let you know that they are with you, protecting you and guiding you.

You will recognize a sign from the unicorns by these characteristics:

- The sign occurs more than once.
- The sign is out of the ordinary or attention-grabbing in another way.
- The sign has a personal meaning to you.
- The sign is timely matched to your prayers or questions that you have communicated to the Divine.

There are two conditions that have to be met before you are able to receive signs from above: (1) you have to be open to their existence, and (2) you have to acknowledge them. Amazing life changes occur when you learn to see and use the messages the unicorns send you in your daily life, in all situations, important or trivial.

Eight Signs from the Unicorns

(1) Feathers

The unicorns are members of the angelic realm and they leave feathers as signs just like angels do. Angel and unicorn feathers are usually small, white and fluffy but they can be more unusual and striking, such as an exotic peacock feather, a colourful parrot feather or a breathtaking eagle feather. The unicorns will leave feathers as a sign that they are watching out for you, as an answer to a question, or as encouragement that you are on the right path. For example, when looking for a new house, you may find a feather on the kitchen floor during a viewing as a confirmation from the unicorns that this is the right location for you at this time in your life.

(2) Flowers

The American poet Ralph Waldo Emerson wrote that "the earth laughs in flowers". Indeed, flowers have always been associated with the beauty, love and inspiration of the divine for as long as humans have appreciated the beauty, harmony and symmetry expressed in each petal. The unicorns have a special affinity with roses and lilies. Roses are the universal symbol of love and are the flower associated with Mother Mary, the archetypical feminine. Unicorns are the familiar, or spirit animal, of Mother Mary. Greek mythology says that Chloris, the goddess of flowers, created the rose from the lifeless body of a nymph with the help of the other gods, including Aphrodite, the goddess of love. The name Eros – the god of love – can be spelt out by rearranging the letters in "rose". These beautiful flowers, their scent or oil are a valuable aid to meditation and prayer. They can ease depression, and release and heal feelings of sorrow, disappointment, fear, jealously and resentment. Roses raise your frequency and open your heart to love, friendship and empathy, encouraging patience and compassion. Rose oil is five times more valuable than gold. It takes 60,000 blooms (180lbs) to produce a single ounce of rose oil. Rose oil has the highest vibrational frequency of any essential oil at 320 megahertz. The unicorns often strew rose petals or leave a rose scent as a sign that they are nearby. Lilies are ancient and universal symbols of the divine, representing the pure, awakened nature of the human consciousness. The lily is the Western equivalent of the Eastern symbol of the lotus, often referred to by its Sanskrit name padma, the most holy flower in Eastern spirituality, because it denotes a pure blossom (spirituality) unsullied by the swamp it grows in (materiality). Unicorns can conjure up a beautiful floral fragrance. It will suddenly surround you, originating from nowhere in particular. Initially very faint, it grows stronger as your unicorn approaches. Then all of a sudden, just as quickly as the scent first appeared, it suddenly vanishes in the fraction of a moment, staying just long enough to transport you into a state of higher consciousness, bliss and divine love.

(3) **Rainbows**

The unicorns are an embodiment of the healing energy of the rainbow. The pure radiant white colour represents the One Source from which all colours originate. The seven colours of the rainbow are equated with seven streams of power, known as the Seven Rays. The Seven Rays flow from the singular white light at the centre and, through this diffusion of light, each ray carries with it one colour from the glorious spectrum of the rainbow. We all have experience of how colours affect our moods, our appetites and many aspects of our daily lives. In the same way, colour also affects our spiritual life, because it *is part of all* life, and each ray, or light frequency, builds a clear passageway to the white light of the centre, from where it first originated. Therefore, no colour can remain in isolation, because it is part of the Greater Whole, and is only an aspect of the diffusion of the One Light and the One Beginning. Equally, no consciousness can remain in isolation, because it is part of the Greater Whole, the One Source and the Universal Mind. When you see a rainbow, the unicorns are reminding you of the interconnectedness of all things. A rainbow inspires you to live life from your authentic self in full consciousness of your divine nature.

(4) **Pearls, Diamonds, Crystals and Other Prisms**

Unicorns embody the essence of the white light of source which refracts into all the colours of the rainbow. This is why they love prisms of all kinds, especially those that occur in nature. This is the deeper reason why unicorns are often depicted near lakes or waterfalls, or in meadows dotted with flowers sparkling with dewdrops at the break of dawn. Water can act as a prism and rainbows are often seen around waterfalls or reflected in dewdrops. Pearls, diamonds and clear quartz crystals also shimmer in all rainbow colours when catching the light. In the same way that you can program a crystal or another object with a wish or intention, you can also use pearls, diamonds and crystals as meditation aids for discovering the deeper nature of an issue or problem you are facing. For this purpose, hold or visualize one of these rainbow representatives in your hands and imagine entering inside its core. Pearls often have insides that appear as lagoons, lakes, or pools, reflecting their aquatic origin, whereas diamonds usually have more earth-based interiors. Stay with the image that comes to your mind in meditation and explore the inner realms of your object of attention. The unicorns sometimes leave messages for you inside these rainbow prisms and exploring their hidden meanings creates a very rewarding meditation experience, which can give you new insights, expand your consciousness and bring you to a state of bliss.

Exercise: Pearl Meditation

Once, I asked my unicorn guide a question on prosperity. For this purpose, I cleared my mind and requested insight into my unicorn guide's visions for me. Then I closed my eyes and asked: "How can I experience the utmost abundance in my life?" In response, I was shown a large black pearl. Black pearls represent wealth and prosperity. I was then told to enter it. As I mentally passed through the walls of the pearl, I found that inside was a beautiful tropical blue lagoon. I experienced myself in the water, playing, enjoying the luxuriant warmth and silky softness of the water. I discovered I had a mermaid's tail, long flowing hair, and the ability to swim like a fish. I felt completely in my element. I started to dive down into the depths of the ocean, feeling like a child on a treasure hunt. I was guided into an underwater grotto and encountered a large, green and pink coloured fish that had an air of authority and significance about him. I wondered what this fish represented, especially as he was not verbally communicating a message to me as I had initially expected. Then I saw a small, maybe six or seven year old boy who I instantly knew was the Greek sea god Poseidon in child form. He was playing with the fish. The fish's energy was very serious, reverent, and earnest whereas the boy's energy in contrast was playful, light hearted, full of wild joy and abandonment. This sequence of images, from the black pearl, to the blue lagoon, to experiencing myself as a mermaid and encountering the colourful fish and the Greek god Poseidon in child form, was given to me one by one, in a seamless, harmonious flow of images. It was like sitting in a cinema, enthralled in the scenes shown on the big screen, experiencing emotions and events as real yet at the same time as a spectator. I understood that the central message was to have fun, enjoy life and immerse myself in it with joyful abandonment as a fish in water but I was still confused by the image of the green and pink fish. When I looked up "fish" in a dream interpretation dictionary, I found the following entry: A fish is a symbol of Christ and may therefore function psychologically as a symbol of your true self. All at once, I realized the significance of the fish shown to me. Green and pink are the colours of the heart chakra. The unicorns were giving me the message that in order to live life most abundantly, I had to live with an open, expanded heart chakra, expressing divine love in my life, gifting the world with my true self. The importance and significance of this message and mission (as displayed in the severity and authority of the fish) was balanced with the loving instruction to be playful, full of laughter and a sense of adventure. In this way, the unicorns gave me the message that a combination of the qualities of divine love in action coupled with a sense of joy, fun and humour is the key to a happy, abundant and fulfilled life.

(5) Coins
Unicorns revel in the abundance of the universe and they want to share the joy and freedom of the true prosperity consciousness as well. Because many people associate financial wellbeing with abundance and prosperity, the unicorns utilize the universal symbol of the coin to assure you that your financial affairs are looked after. Beyond financial security, true prosperity recognizes the ultimate source of all abundance in the divine creator within. Your mind is one with the one mind of all of creation. Any thought you think is simultaneously thought by Divine Mind, the infinite intelligence that creates worlds. Therefore, any thought you think or idea you have, if it is inspired by your authentic self - the spark of the divine within you - must be successful because Divine Mind is always successful. The unicorns sometimes leave things representing prosperity and value for you to find, such as finding money on the street or in unusual places, with the intention of reminding you of the infinite abundance and limitless potential for creative expression in your own mind.

(6) Voices
Sometimes, when your channels are very clear or open, or when there is an upcoming emergency or an excess amount of personal distress (such as a "rock bottom" situation at the height of an addiction which leads to the individual surrendering their ego and asking for help from a higher power) the unicorns will communicate with you through direct verbal communication to ensure that you will hear them. When the unicorns speak, their message and meaning comes through loud and clear and there is no doubt that it pays to listen to what they have to say

to you. Many people hear their name called by a non-physical voice, usually at the time of awakening from sleep because that is the time where we are most open and connected to other dimensions. The voice of God, the angels, the unicorns and all other higher dimensional beings is that of love and wisdom. I am sure that the voice that spoke to me in meditation telling me that I had just received the unicorn energy attunement that I had sought with all my heart came from the angelic dimensions and was probably my unicorn guide, or my guardian angel. When the angelic realms speak to you, the voice, message and meaning is loud, clear, and unmistakable.

(7) Numbers

As discussed earlier, the unicorns frequently use numbers to communicate messages to you. Numbers have an intricate relationship with Creation, an importance that the famous Greek mathematician and philosopher Pythagoras expressed in his claim that numbers are "a living thing" and "the measure of all things," leading to his exploration of "number mysticism" in order to explain the inner workings of the kosmos.[21] Due to their profound nature, numbers are often the most interesting – and at times, mystifying – messages to receive from the unicorns. Sometimes, sequences and patterns reoccurring may seem random events or not make much sense, making you feel perplexed and confused. Often, in these cases, you can sense that there is a deeper meaning to these number patterns reappearing multiple times in your life, and you feel frustrated because you can't seem to crack the code. In these cases, it is good to appreciate the communication as a sign that the higher dimensions are watching over you. If you feel that the message is important, you can ask for further clarifying signs. Check the number meanings in this book or consult books dedicated to metaphysical numerology to decode any number messages you may be getting.

(8) **Gifts**

Unicorn pictures, soft toys, or figurines that are given to you or show up in your life in synchronous ways are very clear signs from the unicorns that they are connecting with you and would like to work with you. If you have already made contact with your unicorn guide, these unicorn gifts are a sign from your guide that you are on the right track and he (or she) is close to you. When I was close to completing this book, I met a lovely girl from Prague, Lilia, who is a spiritual artist (www.lilia.cz). She showed me her newest silk paintings and among them was the most beautiful image of a unicorn. She had painted him in silver white with a golden, spiralling horn, golden hoofs and a golden, curly mane and tail. As soon as I saw the image I could sense that it embodied the true unicorn energy and was obviously made by someone who was in tune with the unicorn vibrations. I went home and could not stop thinking about this beautiful, powerful unicorn silk painting for two days. Finally my husband decided to buy it for me as a present. I placed it on my nightstand, next to my pearls and a large piece of clear quartz crystal that I keep by my bedside. I felt a beautiful, harmonious and peaceful energy flowing from the image, as if a guardian angel was watching over my sleep.

Unicorn Blessing Showers

I have found that, once asked, the unicorns are very eager to help you and give guidance to assist you in living your soul's purpose and experience enhanced joy, love and beauty in your life. Unicorns are giving by nature and they take great delight in sharing, giving and distributing gifts. In meditation, when connecting with my unicorn guide, I have often been surprised with a spontaneous shower of gifts – etheric diamonds, rose petals, golden coins, pearls, jewellery, star dust – raining down on me. The unicorns shoot healing golden and silver star dust from their energy horns to symbolize the peace and love which they distribute freely wherever they appear. The unicorns have fully actualized heart chakras and they realize that when you give something to another, you are in reality giving the gift to yourself, and everyone, because in essence we are all one. They are in a constant flow of unconditional giving because they are connected to the neverending substance of supply within them and all the universe that flows forth without interruption, in a constant stream of joyful givingness. There is nothing which makes them feel happier or more fulfilled than being of service. I see my "unicorn showers" as expressions of their divine love, symbolizing blessings and riches, both spiritual and material.

CHAPTER 8

Ascension with the Unicorns

"As we raise our consciousness and activate our lightbody, we realize we are our own creators made, or making ourselves, in the image and similitude of the one Creator. Indeed, since in a hologram the part contains the whole, we are the one Creator. By learning this truly transformative lesson, we return to unity consciousness while mastering physicality. In other words, we achieve god-realization as the light of soul descends into a divine or soul body healed of duality and freed from the instructional cycle of karma."
— Sol Luckman

What is Ascension?

Ascension means elevating or raising the frequencies or vibrations of our consciousness towards that of the Most High, or God. The unicorns look for people who have a vision beyond their own conditioned ego-selves, who "see the bigger picture", and who wish to be of service to others. It is felt by many that there is a shift in consciousness occurring on this planet at this time. We are moving beyond the dualistic world-view presented to us by our socially and culturally conditioned surface mind, and towards a more mystical or metaphysical understanding of reality. We understand that we are spiritual beings having a physical experience and not physical beings who are biochemically producing a finite consciousness. As more and more people raise their consciousness and start to see who they really are, a momentum is created in the collective consciousness until a tipping point is reached and human consciousness collectively is raised towards a Union with the Divine. Because we are fundamentally all One, each of us being an individualized expression of the one Infinite Intelligence of God, every thought that is thought by one of us is on some level thought by all of us. We really can change the whole world with our thoughts. The unicorns have been drawn to the Earth at this point in time because enough people have raised their vibrations and are sending out a strong white light that has called the unicorns in. They are now teaching and assisting those who are ready. More and more people are being touched by the unicorns and angels.

Brain Waves and Their Related States of Consciousness

The science of brain wave activity holds a key for the understanding of transpersonal, or higher, states of consciousness, in which we experience oneness directly. Electrical activity emanating from the brain is displayed in the form of brainwaves. There are four categories of these brainwaves, ranging from the most activity to the least activity.

When the brain is stimulated and actively engaged in mental activities, it generates beta waves. These beta waves are of relatively low amplitude, and are the fastest of the four different brainwaves. The frequency of beta waves ranges from 15 to 40 cycles a second. Beta waves are characteristic of a mind that is strongly focused on, and engaged in, the external physical world. A person in active conversation is in beta. A debater is in high beta. A person making a speech, or a teacher, or a talk show host, are all in beta when actively involved in their work.

The next brainwave category in order of frequency is alpha. While beta represents arousal, alpha expresses non-arousal. Alpha brainwaves are slower and higher in amplitude. Their frequency ranges from 9 to 14 cycles per second. A person who has completed a task and sits down to rest is often in an alpha state. Someone who takes time out to reflect or contemplate is usually in an alpha state. A person who takes a break from a conference or business activity and goes for a walk in a park, forest or other natural environment is often in an alpha state.

The next category, theta brainwaves, is of even greater amplitude and slower frequency. This frequency range is normally between 5 and 8 cycles a second. A person who has taken time off from an externally focused task and starts to daydream is often in a theta brainwave state. A person who is driving on a high speed road, and discovers that they can't recall the last five miles, is often in a theta state, induced by the "free flowing", automated process of fast, monotonous driving. The repetitive nature of this type of driving compared to driving on a narrow, winding country road expresses itself in the difference between a relaxed theta state and an aroused beta state in order to perform the driving task safely.

Individuals who perform tasks "automatically" for long stretches, often find themselves inspired by ideas during those periods when they are in theta. A person who runs outdoors is often in a state of mental relaxation that is slower than alpha and when in theta, they are prone to a flow of ideas. People often refer to this as "being in the Zone". This experience of flow can also occur in the shower or tub or even while shaving or brushing your hair. It is a state where tasks become so automated that you mentally disengage from them. The ideation that occurs during the theta state is often characterized by an experience of "free flow". This state of consciousness is the result of an absence of censorship, conventionalized thinking, or guilt, which are creations of the conditioned surface mind (or ego-mind) of the beta wave state. The theta (meditative) state is typically a very positive mental state.

The final brainwave state is delta. Here the brainwaves are of the greatest amplitude and slowest frequency. They typically center in a range of 1.5 to 4 cycles per second. Deep dreamless sleep takes place in the lowest frequency, typically 2 to 3 cycles a second. Buddhists call the experience that manifests during this time *The Clear Light of Bliss*. This light is our True Nature at the deepest level but we can only perceive it if we are conscious, or aware, during this time. It is also the light that manifests at the moment of death. Brain death is characterized by zero brain wave activity. The life force energy, or soul, has left the physical body and is no longer occupying it and expressing through it.

When you go to bed and read for a few minutes before attempting sleep, you are likely to be in low beta. When you put the book down, turn off the lights and close your eyes, your brainwaves will descend from beta, to alpha, to theta and finally, when you fall asleep, to delta.

It is a well known fact that humans dream in approximately 90 minute cycles. When the delta brainwave frequencies increase to the frequency of theta brainwaves, active dreaming takes place and often appears very vivid and real to the dreamer. Typically, when this occurs, there is rapid eye movement, which is a characteristic of active dreaming. This is called REM, and is a well known phenomenon. Lucid dreaming is characterized by being "awake", or aware, within the dream. In this way, you can control your thoughts, the dream and its outcome, changing and molding it to reflect the experience you wish to have. When we learn to do this in the dream state, we realize that we are the creators of what we perceive. Our thoughts, as expressed in our brain waves, are the creators of our experience.

When you awake from a deep sleep in preparation for getting up, your brainwave frequencies increase through the different stages of brainwave activity. In other words, if you are in a deep sleep when something awakens you, they increase from delta to theta and then to alpha. When externally focused mental activity returns, they express as beta. If you are in a dream state, which is more likely, especially when you sleep for longer stretches than four hours at night, after which more frequent and longer REM states occur, you are in theta, and progress to alpha and finally beta upon awakening. During the awakening cycle it is possible for you to stay in the theta state for an extended period of five to fifteen minutes, which then allows you to have a free flow of ideas meditating on the activities of the forthcoming day and affirming the outcome as you visualize it.

This time period just before rising and engaging in the activities of the day can be a period of very meaningful and creative mental activity. This is a very productive and useful time for your morning affirmations. Having pen and paper ready by your bedside assists you with writing down your affirmations. You can then repeat and read them to yourself throughout the day which helps you maintain your focus and acts as a constant reminder of your manifestation skills.

In summary, there are four brainwave states that range from the high amplitude, low frequency delta to the low amplitude, high frequency beta. These brainwave states range from deep dreamless sleep to high mental arousal. The same four brainwave states are common to the human species. Men, women and children of all ages experience the same characteristic brainwaves. They are consistent across cultures, nations and countries.

The fact that every human being, regardless of culture, ethnicity, wealth, profession, religion, political or sexual orientation has the same brain wave characteristics, signifying identical stages of consciousness, proves on a scientific level that we all have access to higher (or mystical) states of consciousness, because our brains, and therefore our consciousnesses, function in identical ways. When we utilize the techniques that help us to consciously experience mystical states of consciousness, or a state of oneness, by intentionally introducing alpha and theta brain waves through the practice of meditation, each one of us can experience the Kingdom of God within.

The "Over-Soul"

The evolutionary impulse of the Universe is within each one of us. We all partake of the Divine Intelligence, are animated by it, and are alive by Its Grace. When you realize this great truth, and learn to live from your God-Self, your soul, which is the spark of the Divine within you, many things start to fall into place. You start to become conscious of the subtle patterns and the synchronous flow that direct all life. You start to understand the memories and lifetimes that have formed you into the thought-consciousness you are today. Fear is replaced by faith and anxiety gives way to an inner calm and peace, as you stand observing in wonderment the rich unfolding of life. You start to recognize the significance of every moment and realize that there is meaning in the minutest of events. You connect with everyone and everything in the universe, and recognize the One Mind that unites us all. You unveil the marvellousness that is concealed deep within you, and delight in your newfound splendor. You deliberately shape your life into the endlessly creative expressions it is designed to be, and by doing so we find yourself living your deepest desires and dreams, fulfilling your life's purpose.

In turn, by evolving ourselves, each of us contributes to the evolvement of the collective consciousness.The great American transcendentalist philosopher and poet Ralph Waldo Emerson termed this Oneness of all of creation the "Over-Soul", so called because "within man is the soul of the whole; the wise silence; the universal beauty, to which every part and particle is equally related; the eternal One".[22]

The ancient Vedic tradition of India teaches Advaita, meaning non-duality. The Upanishads are Hindu scriptures that constitute the core teachings of Vedanta. Vedanta is based on two simple propositions: (1) Human nature is divine; and (2) the aim of human life is to realize that human nature is divine. The goal of Vedanta is a state of Self-Realization or Cosmic Consciousness. Historically and currently, it is held that this state can be experienced by anyone, but it cannot be adequately conveyed through language. The Amritabindu Upanishad declares, "Brahman [Ultimate Reality, The Absolute, Universal Intelligence, God] is indivisible and pure; realize Brahman and go beyond all change. He is immanent and transcendent. Realizing him, sages attain freedom, and declare there are no separate minds. They have but realized what they always are. That in whom reside all beings and who resides in all beings, who is the giver of grace to all, the Supreme Soul of the universe, the limitless being — *I am That.* 'I have realized the Self', declares the sage, 'Who is present in all beings. I am united with the Lord of Love'".[23]

I Am That I Am

"I Am That" or "I Am That I Am" is a description or name given to the Source of All Creation, Divine Intelligence, or God, in the Bible as well as in the Vedas. "I Am that I Am" (Hebrew: היהא רשא היהא, pronounced *Ehyeh asher ehyeh*) is a common English translation as given in the King James Bible and others of the response God gave Moses when asked for His name (Exodus 3:14). Hayah means "existed" or "was" in Hebrew; "ehyeh" is the first person singular imperfect form. "Ehyeh" is usually translated as "I will be", since the imperfect tense in Hebrew denotes actions that are not yet completed, as in "Certainly I will be [ehyeh] with thee" (Exodus 3:12). *Asher* is an ambiguous pronoun which can mean, depending on context, "that", "who", "which", or "where". Therefore, although "Ehyeh asher ehyeh" is generally translated into English as "I am that I am", more adequate renderings might be "I will be what I will be" or "I will be who I will be".[24] This interpretation affirms the constant becomingness and newness that constitutes the nature of creation and our identity.

The mystical understanding of All That Is, as experienced in meditation, knows that the non-physical Allness of God is made physically manifest in the Body of God which is the material universe. Everything that is, is an expression of the First Cause, God, the Substance-Principal. It is known as the substance-principal because it is the unchanging reality, the immutable principal that manifests itself as and through substance in the physical universe. Infinite Intelligence, God, is experiencing Itself as, in, and through each one of us. As such, It is always in a joyful, creative state of becoming; forever growing, forever evolving, forever becoming more. Therefore, it is eternally, and joyfully, incomplete (as signified by the use of the Hebrew imperfect form of the verb "to be").

You are Truth

The quantum physicist David Bohm describes the experience of unified consciousness this way, "Even if a hundred people were able to perceive the deepest stratum of reality and tap into the collective mind — the ego would vanish for these people, and they would form a single consciousness, just as the parts of a highly integrated person are integrated as one".[25] The "new" physics has also put forth the theory that our universe (the cosmic body) was whole to begin with and always will be. Science is verifying through its own belief system the same insight that an evolved person can find in their own awareness, namely, that "we are inside truth, and cannot get out of it", as the French philosopher Maurice Merleau-Ponty put it.[26] The sacred Sanskrit text Yoga-Vasistha states that, "Whatever happens, in any form or at any time or place, is but a variation of the One Self-existent Reality".[27]

You Are the Creator of Your Own Experience

We have all been given a great gift, the ability to change our lives by changing our thinking. The way we think determines the way we feel. Most people don't think that newborn children could be the Creator of their own reality, because they are not even talking yet. But the Universe does not respond to your words. The Universe responds to your vibration, and your vibration is an expression of the way you feel. It is scientifically proven that the human heart generates the strongest magnetic field in the body, nearly 5000 times stronger than the brain. This donut-shaped magnetic field extends outside of the physical body and responds to the emotional frequency we generate in our lives. We intuitively know that positive emotions increase health, mental clarity and alertness. Likewise, research shows that negative emotions can affect as many as 1400 biochemical changes in the body, resulting in hormonal imbalances, heart rhythm irregularities, mental confusion, and poor productivity.[28] Even more amazingly, there are studies that suggest that the relationship between the human heart's magnetic frequencies and Earth's magnetic field means that "strong collective emotion has a measurable effect on the earth's geomagnetic field."[29]

So, really, we attract things – people, circumstances, events – into our experience based on the way we feel, which determines our level of vibration. Love, joy, and gratitude are examples of high level vibrations. Anger, hatred, and depression are examples of low level vibrations. And how does this work? It works because we are all related to God. The Absolute created us out of the only substance It had available – Itself! That means that every human being is a manifestation of the Divine. However, it is up to us to accept the gift, the gift of the Divine Relationship. When we yield and allow the flow of Divine Creativity, the Presence of God is given the freedom to live through and as each one of us. The choice is yours to make. Are you ready to "let your light shine", as Jesus urged? Are you willing to claim your birthright, your Divine Inheritance? The unicorns are sent here from the angelic realms to assist you with just that, when you are ready. The fact that you are reading this book right now indicates that you have a strong connection with the unicorns and are a lightworker on this planet, assisting with the task of ascension by healing yourself, being of service and making the "quantum leap" in consciousness to unity consciousness.

You Are a Perfect Idea in the Mind of God

The holy writings of all major religions declare the Oneness of man with the Creator, affirming that humankind is the spiritual image and likeness of God. The Bible emphatically reveals this truth many times over, stating, "God created man in His own image" (Genesis 1:27 KJV). "The spirit of God hath made me, and the breath of the Almighty hath given me life" (Job 33:4 KJV). "Hereby know we that we dwell in Him, and He in us, because He hath given us of His Spirit" (1 John 4:13 KJV). "Be ye therefore perfect, even as your Father which is in heaven is perfect" (Matthew 5:48 KJV). "Ye are the sons of the living God" (Hosea 1:10). "And because ye are sons, God has sent forth the Spirit of His son into your hearts" (Galatians 4:6).

In other words, there is only one son of God, which includes all of humankind, and the spirit of his son, which is the Spirit of Christ, is incarnated in everyone. Therefore, the Bible says that "he [humankind] is the image and glory of God" (1 Corinthians 11:7). The Native American medicine man Rolling Thunder has said, "It's more useful to think of every other person as another you – to think of every individual as a representative of the universe".[30]

Every person is an incarnation of God. "Know ye not that your body is the temple of the Holy Spirit which is in you ... therefore glorify God in your body, and in your Spirit, which are God's" (1 Corinthians 6:19-20 NKJV). This statement is as clear a confirmation of divine incarnation as we could wish for. Since God is the Universal Intelligence, the One Mind, Substance, Power and Presence – in other words, God is All That Is – and since all people are individuals, it follows that each person is an individualized focal point of the Consciousness of the One God.

Many Members, One Body

Each of us is created in the "image and likeness" of God; yet we are all bearers of unique and personal gifts, talents, and preferences, which we have been blessed with by Divine Grace. There are many members of the one body of God, as Paul explains in the Bible (1 Corinthians 12: 12-26). Each part is equally important because it enhances the richness of the universal experience. Paul also explains that those parts that seem deficient or imperfect to us, are most beloved by God, "Nay, much more those members of the body, which seem to be more feeble, are necessary: And those members of the body, which we think to be less honourable, upon these we bestow more abundant honour; and our uncomely parts have more abundant comeliness. For our comely parts have no need: but God hath tempered the body together, having given more abundant honour to that part which lacked" (1 Corinthians 12: 22-24). God is love, and love excludes or rejects nothing; it is always inclusive by nature.

Jesus said, "I and my Father are one" (John 10:30) but "my Father is greater than I" (John 14:28). By this he meant that every person is an extension of God, but no single expression of God can exhaust the Divine Nature. As individuals, we are all expressions of God, yet we are – each and every one of us – completely unique. The Bible verses in 1 Corinthians 12 explain the diversity of spiritual gifts in great detail. I will cite the Bible verses and then provide my own spiritual interpretation that reflects the Truth embodied within them.

1 Corinthians 12 (KJV):

[1]Now concerning spiritual gifts, brethren, I would not have you ignorant. [2]Ye know that ye were Gentiles, carried away unto these dumb idols, even as ye were led. [3]Wherefore I give you to understand, that no man speaking by the Spirit of God calleth Jesus accursed:

and that no man can say that Jesus is the Lord, but by the Holy Ghost.

My Translation:

This is to say that Jesus is only called the Lord because he is a perfect expression of the Holy Spirit. The real Lord is the Divine Spirit within.

⁴Now there are diversities of gifts, but the same Spirit. ⁵And there are differences of administrations, but the same Lord. ⁶And there are diversities of operations, but it is the same God which worketh all in all. ⁷But the manifestation of the Spirit is given to every man to profit withal.

My Translation:

This is a clear confirmation that there is a great diversity of gifts, talents, skills, opinions, governments, social and cultural structures between individual people and individual countries, yet behind all this diversity is the one Spirit, which prospers and blesses everyone and everything.

⁸For to one is given by the Spirit the word of wisdom; to another the word of knowledge by the same Spirit; ⁹To another faith by the same Spirit; to another the gifts of healing by the same Spirit; ¹⁰To another the working of miracles; to another prophecy; to another discerning of spirits; to another divers kinds of tongues; to another the interpretation of tongues:

My Translation:

These are examples of specialized gifts and talents which people are blessed with by the Divine Grace of Spirit (God).

¹¹But all these worketh that one and the selfsame Spirit, dividing to every man severally as he will. ¹²For as the body is one, and hath many members, and all the members of that one body, being many, are one body: so also is Christ.

My Translation:

The One Spirit of God is within all of us. We are all expressions (members) of the One Body of the Physical Manifestation of God.

[13]For by one Spirit are we all baptized into one body, whether we be Jews or Gentiles, whether we be bond or free; and have been all made to drink into one Spirit. [14]For the body is not one member, but many.

My Translation:

Regardless of external appearances ("Jews or Gentiles", "bond or free"), we are all God's most beloved children. The Holy Spirit expresses itself in, as, and through each of us. There is not only one Son of God, no one singular expression of the Divine ("the body is not one member").

[15]If the foot shall say, Because I am not the hand, I am not of the body; is it therefore not of the body? [16]And if the ear shall say, Because I am not the eye, I am not of the body; is it therefore not of the body? [17]If the whole body were an eye, where were the hearing? If the whole were hearing, where were the smelling?

My Translation:

We should not think that we need to be other than we are to become part of God. We are always part of God. We are all needed, in our own unique way.

[18]But now hath God set the members every one of them in the body, as it hath pleased him. [19]And if they were all one member, where were the body? [20]But now are they many members, yet but one body.

My Translation:

The Divine Spirit takes sublime pleasure in each of Its creations. It is the diversity of experiences that makes the Body of God, eternally expanding and evolving through each and every one of us.

[21]And the eye cannot say unto the hand, I have no need of thee: nor again the head to the feet, I have no need of you. [22]Nay, much more those members of the body, which seem to be more feeble, are necessary: [23]And those members of the body, which we think to be less honourable, upon these we bestow more abundant honour; and our uncomely parts have more abundant comeliness. [24]For our comely parts have no need: but God hath tempered the

body together, having given more abundant honour to that part which lacked.

My Translation:

We all need each other, because we are all One. Also the seemingly deficient amongst us, are beloved and blessed by God. As Rabbi Israel Baal Shem-Tov explains, "every human being has a root in the Unity, and to reject the minutest particle of the Unity is to reject it all".31

[25]That there should be no schism in the body; but that the members should have the same care one for another. [26]And whether one member suffer, all the members suffer with it; or one member be honoured, all the members rejoice with it.

My Translation:

We are all united in Spirit. Empathy, sympathy and compassion are important values, because on a deep level we are all One. The collective consciousness is affected by each and every one of us, for better or worse. God is Love, and love knows no separation or rejection, only inclusion.

[27]Now ye are the body of Christ, and members in particular.

My Translation:

Christ is a synonym for the Holy Spirit within. We are all expressions of the Divine. The unique expression of the Divine Mind that is each one of us combines to form an eternally evolving experience in the Mind of God.

The Universal Spirit is individually and uniquely personal to each one of us. Through the God-Mind within, we experience a union with The Absolute which is complete, immediate and dynamic. The great Indian poet and Nobel Prize winner Rabrindranath Tagore has said, "Joy is the realization of the truth of oneness, the oneness of our soul with the world and of the world-soul with the supreme lover [God]".[32] The Bible says, "No man hath seen God at any time; the only begotten Son, which is in the bosom of the Father" (John 1:18). God expresses Itself in as many variations as there are souls. The metaphysician Charles Fillmore explains that the "ability of the individual mind to combine the ideas of Divine Mind in a consciousness of its own makes each of us the "only begotten son", a particular and special creation."[33] No two individuals in the entire universe are exactly alike, because there is always diversity in the ideas appropriated by each individual from Divine Mind.

Does Your Belief System Serve You in Life?

An anthropomorphic, theistic God no longer resonates as we enter the twenty-first century. This is a time of spiritual awakening. As people start to turn to their own minds for answers, the old dogmas and orthodox religious teachings are replaced by self-knowledge and guidance from the Divine self within. God is the conscious, intelligent, creating spirit energy that has been present from the beginning of Creation and manifests in the world of form as creative expression that is endlessly becoming, infinitely evolving. This God energy is *agape* love, the unconditional love of the Divine. Because we are conscious and capable of manifesting *agape* love, humans are co-creators with God and fully responsible for the forms we create; both positive and negative. As co-creators, we must understand that the seeds of *agape* love and the seeds of pain and suffering are embedded in our own hearts.

The pioneering American psychologist and philosopher William James supposed that: "The ultimate test of what a truth means is the conduct it dictates or inspires".[34] His "ultimate test of truth" is very useful in ascertaining the helpfulness of an insight or a philosophy. By applying this test, we find that when we are reacting to life from the level of our conditioned surface mind, we have erratic responses, actions and thoughts, inevitably dependent on external circumstances and situations. When encountering any difficulty or (perceived) negativity, we respond in ways that amplify and affirm the situation, thereby increasing negativity in our experience. There is a saying, "Worrying is like paying interest on money you haven't borrowed". We find that worry attracts more worry, anxiety attracts more anxiety, and unhappiness attracts more unhappiness. The conditioned mind will lock itself into a loop of misery, in the mistaken assumption that it is merely "facing reality head on" and "telling it like it is". In this way, life appears to be a series of random positive and negative experiences, which we have no control over.

The Monkey Mind of Victim Consciousness

In the victim stage of consciousness evolution, we feel powerless in regards to life's circumstances. We feel unable to control our own thoughts and reactions to events so we blame others for behaving, acting and thinking the way they do which we perceive as negatively impacting on our experience. We believe that outside factors are creating our reality and we think, criticize, and judge in accordance with our reflection of "external factors" which impact our life. This is where the term "monkey mind" used in Yogic philosophy originates. The monkey mind is a mind that jumps from thought to thought like a monkey jumps from tree to tree. The monkey mind is not content with being in the present moment, but rather engages in, and is controlled by, the random and often unconscious thoughts that continually arise and pass through.

Living in Duality

As a conscious being, we have two choices. We either manifest the unconscious, conditioned ego-self energies of fear, greed, competitiveness, and jealousy, or we choose to manifest the creative unconditional love energy of our conscious True Self, known in Greek as *agape*. Consciously or unconsciously, we are continuously creating form and experience. The choice we make determines the outcome. Not only does it decide how we feel about others, but also how we feel about ourselves. Do we manifest guilt, shame and fear in our experience by following this train of thought? We may think we are helping by negating (that is, criticizing, judging, or fighting against) what is bothering us. Our intention may be to create peace, harmony and love but if we focus on a lack of these qualities (by fighting against war, poverty, disease, crime) we bring more lack into our experience. It is like telling a child not to run. All it hears is run, so that's what it will do. Like the child, the universe simply does not understand negation, or "no". If you want the child to walk instead of running, it works to say "slow down". The child does as it is told. In the same way, if you desire peace, visualize peace and the universe will affirm your thoughts and manifest more peace in your experience. You always get what you focus on, so by looking at your life, you know exactly what you have been thinking and hence, manifesting. When visualizing or following a train of thought, the question to ask yourself is this: *Will this thought or expression support and enhance life, increase evolutionary complexity, and contribute to the collective evolution of consciousness, or does it go against life, apply simplistic black and white thinking, and conform to the demand of unquestioning obedience to outmoded beliefs and maps of reality?*

Swami Vivekananda advises us, based on the wisdom in the teachings of the Vedanta, that renunciation "really means deification of the world –- giving up the world as we think of it, as we know it, as it appears to us -– and to know what it really is. Deify it; it is God alone. We read at the commencement at one of the oldest of the Upanishads, 'Whatever exists in this universe is to be covered with the Lord'. We have to cover everything with the Lord Himself, not by a false sort of optimism, not by blinding our eyes to evil, but by really seeing God in everything. In life and in death, in happiness and in misery, the Lord is equally present."[35]

Many great writers and thinkers have realized that "good" and "bad" are labels which we apply to things from our human point of view. Shakespeare wrote, "There is nothing either good or bad, but thinking makes it so."[36] Emerson asserted, "Good and bad are but names very readily transferable to that or this; the only right is what is after my own constitution; the only wrong what is against it".[37] It is easy for us to accept that there are things that are labeled as "wrong" or "bad" in one culture, family, or personal worldview, which are not labeled the same in another. Good and bad are not intrinsic qualities, but a reflection of our perspective. The break-up of a relationship may seem bad at the moment, but in the long run we may realize that it was a blessing, leading to better things. The same goes for other things usually termed bad, such as the loss of a job, losing money in the stock market, being passed over for a promotion, and so on. In many cases the real problem is not the event itself, but the way we respond to it, the way we let it define our lives, and the choices we make on the basis of the experience.

But how can we use free choice to our advantage? How do we change our reactions, our impulses? They seem to be deeply ingrained in us, but as Gandhi said: "Your beliefs become your thoughts. Your thoughts become your words. Your words become your actions. Your actions become your habits. Your habits become your values. Your values become your destiny." We can create new habits of thinking and acting. An evolved individual, Martin Luther King, was at an event, when a man spit on him. He did not retaliate. Instead, he wiped off the spit with a handkerchief, and handed it back to the man who had spit on him, saying, "I believe this belongs to you". He had an expanded awareness of love, peace, justice, good will. Because of this, he was able to choose his reaction to the unpleasant event from a higher level of consciousness rather than follow base level impulses. The average individual is impulsively reacting to circumstances based on decisions made by their conditioned surface level mind, rather than choosing to respond from a deeper dimension of their being.

We can experience pain and feel fear, or we can experience pain and feel hope. The condition at that moment is the same, but the feelings and thought vibrations brought forth by the condition are vastly different. The thoughts you think control your feelings and determine the outcome of any situation you find yourself in. By asserting that good must come of this, whether it will be next week, next month, or next year, you set a new cause into motion. Universal Law is neutral, objective and infallible. As soon as you claim your good, it becomes impressed into Divine Law, and the Law must find some way to bring it to you.

To be clear, this does not imply that we have to experience pain, suffering and unwanted situations in order for us to learn and manifest our desires. We can learn and grow just as much from joyful and healthy experiences. However, if undesired conditions manifest, our reaction determines the outcome. To assist us in focusing on the lesson in the unwanted situation, we concentrate our energy on feeling positive and hopeful. In the face of adversity, we are always free to affirm "goodness will result from this!" Your vision will unfailingly manifest, in accordance with the spiritual laws of the universe. In this way, we can transform any situation that is undesirable, negative, or hurtful into a force for good in our lives.

Be Like the Oyster: How to Transform Aggravation into Beauty

There is a powerful Buddhist practice called "Transforming Difficulties Into The Path". The Path referred to here is the path of Spiritual Growth, the evolution of consciousness; in Buddhist terms, the Path to Enlightenment. It is the same principle that the humble oyster applies. When a grain of sand irritates the soft flesh of the oyster, what does it do? It protects itself by creating a beautiful pearl around the grain of sand. Its defense mechanism has created something unique and stunningly beautiful in response to an aggravation, an irritation, or undesired experience.

It is important to remember not to allow ourselves to develop a guilt complex around negative things that happen in our lives that seem to be out of our control, such as parental alcoholism or earth quakes, for example. Regardless of what is happening in our lives, we always have a choice about how we allow these things to affect us, what decisions we make as a result of the experience, and what truths we choose to believe about Life and God as a result of them.

But… If God is Good, How Can Evil Exist?

God is Love. You are Love. Only Love is Real. On a deep level, we know this to be the profound truth of our being; but unfortunately, there are many ways in which we do create and allow things while in a human body on the earth which do not reflect our Source. Just as we are each creating our own personal reality, we are also participating in creating our global reality. Whatever attitudes and beliefs are held most strongly and dominantly in the mass consciousness will, according to Law, be manifested as the collective reality of our world. Unresolved conflict and pain, held in the consciousness of millions of people around the world, is reflected back to us in the form of war, hostile relations between countries, violence and fear in our environments and relationships, and in our collective disregard for the rights of other human beings and the physical harmony and equilibrium of our planet.

When confronted with a situation they do not wish to experience, or they do not wish others to be afflicted by, often people then ask: "How can God let that happen?" People frequently get angry, frustrated or hopeless when confronted with things which seem unjust, cruel, or inhumane. Here, we arrive at the heart of the matter. As human beings, we are endowed with free will, and free choice. That includes the choice to go against nature, against love, against God.

Because everything is Oneness, and The Absolute is everything, there can be no two forces of Good and Evil, no duality of Light and Darkness. Taken to its logical conclusion, this means that we cannot blame our destructive actions, behaviors or choices on anything outside of ourselves. So, it is not a matter of God letting bad things happen; what is really happening is that we are choosing to think and act in ways that go against God, against life. The great psychic Edgar Cayce encapsulated this profound truth with the words: "As has ever been the experience of each soul; that the Law is One, the Source is One! And those that seek other than that find tribulation, turmoils, confusion."[38] The Buddha said, "Intrinsically all living beings are Buddhas, endowed with wisdom and virtue, but because their minds have become inverted through delusive thinking they fail to perceive this".[39]

Free Choice and Free Will: What do They Really Mean?

This brings us to the philosophical concept of evil (also called darkness, or negativity) as separation from God. We are free to choose our thoughts (freedom of choice) and we are free to turn away from God (free will). In other words, our thoughts are free and we will ourselves into being and experiencing with our thoughts. Any negative thought or action, big or small, separates us from the Divine Creative Force, which always promotes life, love and joy. With every life-negating thought of lack, anger or hatred, we are denying our own essence. Whenever there is a discord between what we truly are, and what we are thinking or doing, the demonstration that results will be negative, painful or destructive. For example, our true essence is love, therefore, when we engage with our spouse in ways that are unloving, judgmental or controlling, then communication will be unharmonious and we are putting a strain on the marriage, which may eventually lead to a break-down of the relationship, resulting in divorce. A person who is One with the Love-Power-Intelligence-Creativity that they truly are, will not kill or abuse or harm or hurt or destroy any part of God's Creation in any way. When we listen to our higher guidance, as expressed in our higher self, and transmitted by the angels, unicorns and ascended masters (souls who are evolved in consciousness), we start to follow our soul path and begin manifesting our life choices in co-creation with the divine. Edgar Cayce, the famous American psychic, explained that the activities of a soul (or entity, as Cayce called the individuated stream of consciousness) in the material world were made either "good or bad or indifferent, depending upon the entity's application of self towards that which is the ideal manner for the use of time, opportunity and the *expression* of that for which each soul enters a material manifestation".[40] In other words, the application and expression of our life path as reflected in the purpose of our soul for incarnation must be followed for our actions to be good, that is fulfilling, beneficial and satisfactory. When our thoughts and actions reflect the broader perspective of our higher self, we always feel good. This is an easy way to check if we are "on track". A discord in the perception of Source and our own thoughts will always manifest as a feeling of dis-ease, fear, guilt, shame, or hopelessness. We can then deliberately choose to find thoughts that feel better and in this way bring ourselves into alignment with Source once more.

The Angels and the Unicorns do not have free will, meaning that they do not live in the world of duality and so cannot choose to act in ways that go against God, or love. They are always united with the Divine; and their every thought, word and action is an expression of divine love and divine wisdom. They are ascended beings who have actualized unity consciousness and are now showing the way to us.

CHAPTER 9

How to Live Your Life's Purpose

"Yes! To this thought I hold with firm persistence;
....the last result of wisdom stamps it true:
He only earns freedom and existence who daily conquers them
anew."
- Johann Wolfgang von Goethe

<u>Gifting the World with the Real You</u>

Each one of us brings a complete personality, with different temperaments, talents, and gifts into this world. The moment we hit the ground, however, everyone tries to change us. Even the most well meaning parents will try to mold their children in some way. Very often, by the time we are adults, our soul level personality will be buried underneath a conditioned personality of our own, mostly unconscious, creation.

Through meditation, you can realize your union with the eternal life of God, in the process of which you will awaken to our true soul personality. The unicorns say that this is the moment when you will finally be living Christ's instruction to *let your light shine.* Understanding and recognizing your true soul-type, your God-Self, will lead to genuine self-acceptance. When someone attacks you or criticizes you, you will rest peacefully in the knowledge that, "This is the way I am. Divine Grace has created me this way and blessed me with many gifts to bless my fellow humans in return. I am here to share and embody the love of God in my own unique and specialized way. I am wanted and needed by all the Universe, because there is *no one* who can be, do, and express what I can be, do, and express".

The unicorns understand that not everyone knows what their talents really are. They say: *"Many people go through life, never feeling fulfilled, because they believe that they have to work long, hard hours in a job they do not enjoy just to 'make ends meet'. That is not a life. It is barely an existence! Do you really believe that this is the life that the Divine Source imagines for you, Its most beloved Child?"*

They have the following advice for uncovering your authentic self: *"To begin to get to know the Real You, the You that God intends you to be, the You that God knows you to be, ask yourself these questions: 'What are the things I love to do, that bring me joy, fill me with passion and take me into a timeless space of pure creative flow?' 'What are the talents I am blessed with?' 'What things come naturally to me?' 'What skills have I developed that I enjoy sharing?' 'What makes my heart sing?' 'What activity could I engage in all day and never feel bored?' 'If I could be or do anything and money was no object, what would I choose?' These are all questions that can lead you to discover your soul purpose."*

Japanese Zen roshi Taizan Maezumi explains that, "Regardless of whether we realize it or not, we are always in the midst of the Way. Or, more strictly speaking, we are nothing but the Way itself".[41] You are important and you are needed, just the way you are. Let go of any preconceived ideas that in order to have a purpose in life you have to do earth-shattering things such as discovering the cure for cancer or eradicate world hunger. These are all worthwhile accomplishments but they are outer accomplishments and have no importance to the inner life. When you frame your questions of soul purpose in the larger context of Divine life, the answers come readily. The historian Harold Whitman advises us: "Don't ask yourself what the world needs; ask yourself what makes you come alive. And then go and do that. Because what the world needs is people who have come alive."

A Liberating Shift In Perception

The unicorns teach: "*You have not incarnated with the desire to tell God or the Universe what to do, or when and how to do it. Likewise, you never intended to come forth into physicality merely to order material accessories from the Cosmos. It is time to awaken from the slumber and remember your true self. You are a magnificent creator here on earth. When you chose this form, you knew that in order to live your life's purpose, all you needed to do was to be an open vessel for what God was already doing.*"

There is a cosmic pattern of life, a level of order and reality beyond the human life experience. Each of us is a composite spiritual idea, containing within us every single idea that the Universal Mind has ever thought. You are here for a reason. How can you discover your life's purpose?

How to Discover Your Soul Purpose

In order to live the life your soul intended, you merely have to open yourself up to begin to live out God's vision for your life. The vision is already accomplished in the mind of God. It is already a complete idea in Spirit, so you do not have to pray for its success or accomplishment. Divine Mind is *always* successful. All you need is the willingness and openness to be an effective instrument for the vision of God.

Answer these questions in writing, filling in as much detail as you can and picture yourself in your perfect, ideal life. Smell, taste, feel, experience it as if you are right there and it is already reality. Your vision will come to fruition much quicker if you can do this exercise daily.

1. How does Source envision Itself as my life?
2. How can I express a greater degree of truth with the skills and talents which I have been given?
3. How can I shine brighter, express myself and help others?
4. When do I feel good and in tune with myself and nature?
5. What do I love to do?

6. What do I get enthusiastic, focused, happy about?
7. What makes me forget time?

The unicorns say to me:

"The celestial music is always playing; by tuning your body and mind (your receivers) into the divine frequency, you become the station that plays the music of the heavens here on earth."

When you shift your perception of reality towards God's idea for you, which is your soul purpose, you discover that God's idea is infinite and eternally expressing. There is no end to the growth. There is no stagnation. You just become a bigger and bigger space for It to express through. When you consciously shift your perceptions and lift your vibrations to allow your God-Self to express through you, you are letting the presence of God use you, which is what all the great mystics have done. They did not walk the Earth telling God what to do or what they wanted. They lived to glorify God. The Bible gives very clear instructions to live life from your authentic self; and not to seek approval from the world: "And be not conformed to this world: but be ye transformed by the renewing of your mind, that ye may prove what is that good, and acceptable, and perfect, will of God". (Romans 12:1-2) Base your choices in life on what makes *you* happy, not on other people's expectations of you or the need of approval from others. Only *you* - the higher self or divine spark in you - can truly know why you chose to come here into this physical form at this time.

We realize the strength in surrendering. When we understand the laws of the universe, we hold the key to manifestation but we have not yet entered through the gate of soul purpose. We can manifest whatever we wish for but lasting happiness will elude us until we start living our soul purpose. We can only manifest our soul purpose if we are acting from our higher self, in alignment with Source. The key to manifestation lies in the recognition that there is a power for good in the universe and we can use it. We pass through the gateway of soul purpose when we surrender our ego-mind desires to our higher self, allowing the power that creates worlds to use us.

In this way, you become a living embodiment of God's ideas by letting God work through you. Nothing feels better than raising your awareness towards a mystical union with God, because by knowing Who You Are, on a soul level, you are increasing your freedom and your creativity to ever expanding degrees. The dreams, desires and visions for your life, which result from this mystical communion with the Divine, are God's ideas for you. When you enter into a mystical state of being, and let your God-Self express through you, in all that you live, you are fulfilling your heart's desire, which is *the same thing* as God's will for you.

Let Your Light Shine

You are a child of the Divine, an individualized expression of the one cosmic mind of God. God does not sit on a cloud up in the sky somewhere, in a distant place called heaven. The Bible affirms, "All things were made by Him; and without Him was not any thing made that was made. In Him was life; and the life was the light of men. And the light shineth in darkness; and the darkness comprehended it not" (John 1:3-5 KJV). This clearly means that we all have the light of God within us; but are conditioned into limited and erroneous thinking (darkness) where we fail to perceive the Divine Light in ourselves and others. Likewise, the Buddha said: "Be a lamp unto yourself. Don't search for light anywhere else; the light is already there, the fire is already there. Just probe a little deeper into your being; enquire. Maybe much ash has gathered around the fire... Just probe deep inside and you will find the spark again. And once you have found a single spark inside you, you will become a flame, soon you will be a fire... a fire that purifies, a fire that transforms, a fire that gives you a new birth and a new being." You are a light being, a child of God and as such, there are no limits to what you may become. In Psalm 82, God says, "I have said, Ye are gods; and all of you are children of the most High." (Psalm 82:6) Learning, evolving and growing does not require you to "follow" or emulate someone else. Find your "I Am". I Am represents a person who has God presence, who has realized their Union with God, and who recognizes their relationship with God.

I Am That I Am is the statement of who-you-are at any point in your journey. Own and take responsibility for your personal journey as a part of the Universe, as a child of God. It belongs to you, and no one else. Do not give away your power to others by following conditioned, limited beliefs and rules. Recognize them for what they are, delusions based on fear born out of separation from God, and release them. Only accept ideas which promote harmony, peace and joy. The Christian existentialist philosopher Paul Tillich has remarked that the "most intimate motions within the depths of our souls are not completely our own. For they belong also to our friends, to mankind, to the universe, and to the Ground of all being, the aim of our life".[42] You must never underestimate the powerful impact you have on the collective consciousness, whether you take responsibility for it or not. It takes a relatively small number of individuals moving into alignment with universal forces to have a great impact on our global reality. By cultivating our own individual growth process, we affect others profoundly, and we act as a catalyst for the evolution of the mass consciousness. Through our personal efforts, insignificant as they may sometimes seem to us, we really can change the world.

Let, Don't Get

We see evolution taking place in physical form in our world through the emergence of new ideas, changing religious beliefs, the inception of new social and political systems, and the invention of new technologies. The evolutionary impulse of the Universe is expressed in each individual. Life feels joyful, exciting, magical, when we focus on letting rather than getting. Being in the flow of Divine energy is a matter of letting or allowing answers, inspiration and right action to come, opening up and allowing them in, as opposed to getting these things by force or through anxiety, worry and competitiveness. You can think of prayer as you talking to God, while intuition is God talking to you. When you listen to the Divine voice within, you are allowing God's all-knowing inspiration to guide your life.

The power of allowing can be applied to every area of your life that may have previously seemed difficult. Difficulty is a sign that you may be resisting instead of allowing. For example, you can *let* your body be healthy instead of trying to *get* into shape. This shift in consciousness invites the power of listening to what the body needs and enjoys and then simply providing it without resistance. There is no answer outside of you, no process to undergo except deep listening and the willingness to be available to the answer that you already have. Seen from this broader perspective, there is no need to consult diet and nutrition manuals, anti-ageing guides, or the latest aerobic DVD. *You* are the expert on the subject of *you*.

I'm Dying for a Steak!

I had a powerful experience of the wisdom of the higher self on the subject of nutrition in the aftermath of my cancer treatment. After losing a lot of weight, strength and muscle as a result of six months of constant nausea, loss of appetite, and vomiting I was in a shape of physical frailty that was of great concern to those close to me. I would sit in front of my plate and simply could not bring myself to put any food in my mouth. I now know that by that point my mind associated food with misery because for so long I had been unable to eat, or keep any food inside of me. My mother, who was looking after me, at this stage was frantic with worry and was trying anything to help me regain my appetite, strength and vitality -- from vitamins and supplements to high caloric meal substitutes. My body rejected all of those. At this point I had been a vegetarian for 13 years and a vegan for eight. I was very strict with my diet before becoming ill, taking great care to buy organic, fresh, whole foods and preparing them for (what I believed to be) maximum energy and goodness. Sitting at the dinner table one night, experiencing intense frustration because I could not bring my body-mind to accept the food that was offered on the plate, I had a moment of revelation. It was as if all the cells in my body were forming one voice and what they were saying came as a huge surprise, both to me and everybody around me who knew of my vegetarian convictions. What my cells said was: "We would really like to eat a steak!" Naturally, my mother was overjoyed that I showed any interest in food at all, and very kindly bought me the most expensive, organic, outdoor reared, grass fed piece of beef that she could get her hands on. That small steak was the first real meal I had in six months! All the cells in my body felt energised, vitalized and nourished. It was really most amazing. That episode taught me so many things about my body, nutrition and holding on to strict intellectual beliefs. Now I base all my food choices on what my body is requesting *that day*. I eat a much more varied diet as a result, because my body's needs change constantly. My one guiding "food principle" is that I bless and enjoy everything I eat and drink, whether it is a piece of chocolate, a glass of champagne or a plate of raw vegetables and salad. I am conscious of how food production affects the environment and also the quality of energy within the food, so I choose food where the producers (people and animals) are treated with respect, which in most cases means fair-trade and organic products. Ultimately, I feel that *what* we eat is important, but not as important as *how* we eat.

I have lived in Germany, England, Spain, Malaysia and the United States, and have travelled extensively through North America, Western and Central Europe and South-West Asia. The one thing countries with the longest life expectancies, such as Japan, Spain, France, Italy, and Greece, all seem to have in common is that food is celebrated and enjoyed and is much more integrated into the daily ritual of life than in the United Kingdom and the United States, which both have lower life expectancies than all of these countries. Although smoking and red wine (especially at mealtimes), both labelled as "bad for health", are much more prevalent in these societies than in the United States for example, people in these cultures still live longer and healthier – and I would venture to say, from personal experience, they have more fun and experience less neurosis around food as well. The Italians have even coined a phrase for their celebratory attitude toward life. They call it "la dolce vita", the sweet life. I love that expression. It shows love, joy, and gratitude for life. I think this is the most beneficial way to approach life and all questions of lifestyle. Live, love and enjoy life. That is the most important thing. There are many ways to do that and *You* - the broader perspective or higher consciousness part of you - know what is best for *you*. Overall, I believe the most important thing is to be kind, grateful and connected – to yourself, to other people, and to the Earth.

Unicorn Advice for Healthy Living

I asked the unicorns for their advice on how to live healthily, keep in good shape, and eat well. They responded by teaching me what they call "Recipe for Guilt-Free Living". Basically, they said that if you do *one* thing to live a healthier life then make sure that you never feel guilt for anything you eat, or choose, or do. Any time you put anything in your mouth, reflect for a moment and get in touch with your emotions. How do you feel at this moment? Do you feel empty, unworthy, a sinner? Do you see the food or drink in your hand as an enemy, a "bad" thing, something you will regret later? Whenever you feel a negative vibration around anything you are about to ingest, or engage in, take a step back and search for the reason behind the guilt. Maybe you have been taught that chocolate is "naughty" – you still enjoy eating it but feel you shouldn't, and then when you do "give in" you feel frustrated and guilty about your "lack of willpower". There are two ways to deal with this if you follow the unicorns' Guilt-Free Diet – you don't eat the chocolate, and feel good; or you eat the chocolate, and feel good. The outcomes of both will be the same, according to the wisdom of the unicorns, but you *have to feel good* about your choice. The unicorns say that if you practise this technique of "Guilt-Free Living", making sure that you feel good about every single choice you make in your life, no matter what it is, you will see amazing results in just one week.

Let Go and Let God

Thoughts are energy – some high energy and some low. This means that every thought you think has the power to strengthen or weaken you. In other words love, tolerance and forgiveness make you a stronger person; while anger, fear and guilt make you weaker. Most of us have some resistance to "surrendering" to our higher self, love, and God because our ego fears "handing the power over". Eleanor Roosevelt once said, "You gain strength, courage and confidence from every experience in which you really stop to look fear in the face. You must do the thing you think you cannot do". Most of us interpret this as referring to some courageous action to be taken or fear bravely confronted. However, it can equally apply to the fear of living without resistance. You can learn to reside in a deep trusting place where love is set free and inspiration and powerful intention *let* more accomplishment come into being than you have ever imagined or witnessed before. Frantic external action, bustle and constant *getting* are the diversions that stymie real accomplishment from ever being birthed. With this truth in mind, *letting* is a stimulating and empowering space to settle into. *Letting* means the power of opening to the grand expansiveness of God and standing in the simplicity of being guided. If you listen deeply, with your inner hearing, you may also find that this is the one thing you think you cannot do. The answer is – don't think, do.

Ultimately, right attitudes lead to right actions, right actions lead to right living, and right living leads to fulfilment. We are the sum total of the experiences we have created in the past and what we can now create. We exist in the continuous flow of our creations, and the flow is changed and varies moment by moment under the influence of these creations. While it is possible to make instantaneous great leaps in positive thinking, most of us grow one step at a time. Your belief structure now -- your attitudes, emotions, goals and hopes now -- will help counter any negative creations of the past, and will help you project a more positive future. Since you are at the helm, at the leading edge of thought, piloting your continuous flow of creation, you can direct it wherever you wish.

Once you feel connected to your purpose, new doors will open and marvellous things will begin happening. How do you know that you have found the right purpose? You know you are *on purpose* when you truly enjoy pursuing it, when it feels "right" and you can't wait to get to work. When you truly know what you want, you can see it, you can feel it; it is as though you have it already. When this is the case, the law of attraction which states that "that which is like unto itself is drawn" or simply "like attracts like" ensures that the vision *must* be brought into your experience because you are a perfect vibrational match for it.

Your personal success then becomes effortless because it is emanating from true inner life force and is not a result of using elbow power and selfish tactics to steamroller over people and climb the ladder of life by brute force.

Listen to the unicorns whispering in your ear:

Don't push the river. It flows by itself. Enter the current and ride the wave. Dance with life without resistance. Grace is prevalent everywhere.

Ask and You Shall Receive

When you surrender to God's vision for you, what you really do is get into alignment with who-you-really-are. You are a part of God, an extension of the infinite intelligence of the universe. You do not give up your individual power or your highest intentions. Rather you align your entire being consciously, by choice, with the very highest, brightest Goodness of God. When you are blended with who-you-really-are, when you are living from the God consciousness within, then anything you ask for will be in tune with God's vision for you.

How do you know that you are in alignment with who-who-really-are? You know because you feel good. Your emotions are your built-in guidance system to discover your authentic self. The All always gives because it is Its nature to do so. The universe always says yes. In order to receive, you have to be in a state of allowing. When you are living from your authentic self, you feel joyful, inspired, creative. In other words, you are in a state of allowing. So, in order to receive the Goodness that The All has prepared for you in accordance with your wishes, you only have to come into alignment with this Good, and allow it. God will always provide exactly what you ask for: "Or what man is there of you, whom if his son ask bread, will he give him a stone? Or if he ask a fish, will he give him a serpent? (Matthew 7:9-11)

You are God's most beloved child, which is another way of expressing the fundamental truth that we are all individuated outpourings, sparks, extensions or emanations of the one infinite divine consciousness, temporarily clothed in physical form. Because you and God, the Creative Principle, are One, when you accept the full potential and power of this relationship, everything that you wish for can freely flow into your experience. Your prayers are never not answered, your desires are never ignored and your wishes are never overlooked. God always gives. But you don't always receive, because you don't always allow.

You Have to Believe It to See It

You have to believe it to see it. Jesus explains this "secret" very clearly when he says, "And all things, whatsoever ye shall ask in prayer, *believing*, ye shall receive" (Matthew 21:22). The importance of confidence, faith or belief is again stressed in 1 John: "And this is the confidence that we have in him, that, if we ask any thing according to his will, he heareth us: And *if we know that he hear us*, whatsoever we ask, we know that we have the petitions that we desired of him." (1 John 5:14-15)

In order to allow the flow of goodness in your life you must believe that it is there. You cannot see anything if you are looking in the other direction. When you focus on lack, or doubt, or worry then you are not looking in the direction of your Good, you are not looking with the eyes of who-you-really-are and you, at that moment, have consciously separated yourself from the eternal flowing stream of Divine Love, of God. God always hears you ("we know that he hear us") because any thought you think is also thought by the universal mind. When you are aware of this union, you consciously co-create with the Divine. "If ye abide in me, and my words abide in you, ye shall ask what ye will, and it shall be done unto you." (John 15:7)

Christ stressed the importance of aligning yourself with the higher consciousness, the Christ-Mind within, in order to consciously create and allow the experience of Goodness into your experience. "Verily, verily, I say unto you, Whatsoever ye shall ask the Father *in my name* [in Christ/ higher consciousness], he will give it you." (John 16:23)

Our innermost desires and God's plan for us, our soul purpose, are one and the same. They must be, because we are an outpouring of the limitless love of God. Our desires exist because universal mind has thought them first. *"For your Father knoweth what things ye have need of, before ye ask him."* *(Matthew 6:7-8 KJV)* Infinite Intelligence *loves* experiencing Itself as you. Life is supposed to be fun. Life is joy. Life is laughter. Life is love. If you are having fun and are happy, the things that you desire come into your life faster, not because they weren't there to begin with, but because now you are allowing them in. Remember, "for God so loved the world that he gave" (John 3:16). God is the divine givingness of the universe. The divine flow requires only one thing from you: your consent to be a receiving channel. It is like the water faucet that needs to be opened in order for the water to flow out freely.

Use the following exercise to help you open up to becoming a clear conduit of divine mind; or, as the mystic Joel Goldsmith put it, "being a transparency for God".

Meditation: "Living In The Divine Flow"

Find a quiet space where you can sit undisturbed and centre yourself within. Visualize your skin becoming completely transparent so that all your muscles and tendons show through. Now imagine that all your muscles become transparent and you can now see your bones and organs show through. Now all your bones and organs become transparent, revealing all of your blood vessels and nerves. Now all your blood vessels and nerves become transparent, leaving you completely transparent, a crystalline human shell. Now focus your mind on God, the Absolute Consciousness of the Universe. Invite it to flow through your transparent being into this world. Relax and allow this flow of God to pour through every luminous atom of you into the world. You are a clear window, a pristine outlet, a conduit of the Divine. As this substance flows through your being, set your intention in love, feeling its harmony with your inner being. Pouring through you into your whole life.

CHAPTER 10

The True Nature of Unicorns and Other "Mythological Creatures"

"Do you know, I always thought unicorns were fabulous monsters, too? I never saw one alive before!"
"Well, now that we have seen each other," said the unicorn, "if you'll believe in me, I'll believe in you."
- Lewis Carroll (Through The Looking Glass)

Vibrational Dimensions: "Nothing Rests, Everything Moves, Everything Vibrates"

According to Hermetic teachings, as taught in the *Kybalion*, a classic esoteric self-help book that was first published in 1908, we live in a vibrational universe that consists of Three Great Planes. Each of the Three Great Planes is subdivided into seven minor planes which in turn consist of seven sub-divisions each. Although the human intellect likes to compartmentalize for convenience of thought and study, you should remember that the divisions are arbitrary since the planes and sub-divisions blend into each other. The planes and sub-categories are differentiated by frequencies of vibration, from the slowest and most dense, to the highest and most spiritual. The Three Great Planes are the Physical Plane, the Mental Plane, and the Spiritual Plane. The Great Physical Plane and its seven minor planes includes everything physical and material. Since hermetics recognize matter as a particularly dense, slowly vibrating form of energy, three of the seven minor planes of the Great Physical Plane relate to energy.

The seven Minor Physical Planes are as follows:
1. The Plane of Matter (A)
2. The Plane of Matter (B)
3. The Plane of Matter (C)
4. The Plane of Ethereal Substance
5. The Plane of Energy (A)
6. The Plane of Energy (B)
7. The Plane of Energy (C)

The Plane of Matter (A) includes matters in liquids, solids, and gas. The Plane of Matter (B) comprises higher vibrational forms of matter such as radioactive waves and particles. The Plane of Matter (C) involves the most subtle Matter, which science cannot adequately measure. The Plane of Ethereal Substance is composed of ether, which is the medium for energy waves, and fills all universal space. Next highest in vibrational frequency is the Plane of Energy (A), which includes heat, light, electricity, magnetism, and attraction forces (i.e. gravity, cohesion and chemical affinity). The Plane of Energy (B) relates to what is known as "Nature's Higher Forces", which are higher forms of energy not yet discovered by science. They conduct the energy of mental phenomena, such as telepathy. The Plane of Energy (C) includes energy in such high states of organization that it has many of the characteristics of "life". This energy is only known to those beings on the Spiritual Plane and to those who know and experience this plane while still living on the earth.

The seven minor planes of the Great Mental Plane are:
1. The Plane of Mineral Mind.
2. The Plane of Elemental Mind (A)
3. The Plane of Plant Mind.
4. The Plane of Elemental Mind (B)
5. The Plane of Animal Mind.
6. The Plane of Elemental Mind (C).
7. The Plane of Human Mind.

The Plane of Mineral Mind relates to those entities that animate the minerals, crystals, and chemicals. The material forms of these entities are atoms and molecules, just as your human body is the physical form of you. These entities can be called "souls", according to Hermetics, and they vibrate at slightly faster rates than the living energy of the highest physical plane. Most people do not sense the mind, soul, or life within the mineral kingdom but many mystics, crystal healers and meditators recognize this existence, while modern science is also moving rapidly towards the view of Hermetics, in this respect. Molecules, atoms, and particles have their likes and dislikes, and attractions and repulsions. Some scientists are now saying that the emotions of atoms differ from those of humans only in degree. Mystics know this to be a fact.

The Plane of Elemental Mind (A) includes the most basic elemental beings that are invisible to ordinary human senses but nevertheless play their role in the drama of the Universe. Their degree of intelligence is between that of the mineral and chemical entities on the one hand, and the entities of the plant kingdom on the other.

The Plane of Plant Mind is composed of the kingdoms of the Plant World. Plants have life, mind, and soul. The Plane of Elemental Mind (B) involves higher vibrating and more intelligent elementals than the (A) Elemental Plane. The Plane of Animal Mind comprises the beings, entities, or souls animating the animal forms of life. The Plane of Elemental Mind (C) are the highest vibrational, and most intelligent, elemental beings, such as fairies, elves, leprechauns, and such. The Plane of Human Mind is the human life and mentality. This plane, like the others, has seven sub-categories from the slowest vibrational rate of low intelligence, to the highest frequency of spiritual wisdom and intelligence. The human race has spent millions of years evolving in intelligence to reach the fourth subdivision of vibration and intelligence. Some advanced souls are vibrating on the levels of the fifth, sixth, or seventh sub-divisions. Some humans even vibrate at a rate of the lower levels of the next highest plane, the Great Spiritual Plane. Humans who have reached the level of adept or avatar are at the lowest subdivisions of this plane. Above them are the angels, archangels, ascended masters, and deities. These unseen divinities and angelic helpers work tirelessly and powerfully in the process of evolution and cosmic progress. They also help and intervene with human affairs.

Even the highest of these advanced beings is still a creation existing in the Mind of The All, or God, and is still subject to universal laws. According to the hermetic axiom "as above, so below", the universal laws, and the Seven Hermetic Principles, apply to all levels of existence equally. The Seven Hermetic Principles are explained in the *Kybalion* as the Principle of Mentalism (*"The All is Mind; The Universe is Mental"*), the Principle of Correspondence (*"As above, so below; as below, so above"*), the Principle of Vibration (*"Nothing rests; everything moves; everything vibrates"*), the Principle of Polarity (*"Everything is Dual; everything has poles; everything has its pair of opposites; like and unlike are the same; opposites are identical in nature, but different in degree; extremes meet; all truths are but half-truths; all paradoxes may be reconciled"*), the Principle of Rhythm (*"Everything flows, out and in; everything has its tides; all things rise and fall; the pendulum-swing manifests in everything; the measure of the swing to the right is the measure of the swing to the left; rhythm compensates"*), the Principle of Cause and Effect (*"Every Cause has its Effect; every Effect has its Cause; everything happens according to Law; Chance is but a name for Law not recognized; there are many planes of causation, but nothing escapes the Law"*), and the Principle of Gender (*"Gender is in everything; everything has its Masculine and Feminine Principles; Gender manifests on all planes"*).

How Do We Know About Other Dimensions of Consciousness?

As shown in the Hermetic model of vibrational levels of existence, or consciousness, all beings are enfolded, created and held within the Infinite Love and Infinite Intelligence of God. Angels, Unicorns, Pegasus, Mermaids, Fairies, Sylphs, Leprechauns, Elves, and all other elemental or ascended beings are all part of God, just as every human is part of God. We simply vibrate at different frequencies. Humans' physical senses do not have a wide range of perception and can only recognize vibrations that are close to their own. Few people can see fairies, or angels, or recognize the consciousness-energy vibration within crystals and gemstones.

However, quantum physics has shown that we cannot possibly perceive everything in the universe with our physical senses, and the things we do perceive vary according to who is looking and from which perspective we are watching. We, for the most part, cannot perceive God, or angels, or unicorns, or mermaids with our physical senses but we cannot see radio waves either and yet they are there because when we tune into them using a receiver that is built for that specific purpose, we can suddenly hear them. We can sense, perceive and experience other dimensions of reality in meditation and in altered states of consciousness, when are we using "receivers" tuned into different frequencies, waves and vibrations that are not confined to a three-dimensional reality interpreted through the filter of our physical senses.

The Vibrational Nature of Unicorns

This is how the unicorns themselves describe their Beingness, their soul purpose and their mission here on Earth:

"Greetings to all beloved manifestations of the Creator on the Earth. We honour, love and respect you. We are sending our light to your aid now to enhance your inner light and remove limitations from your life. We come as the unicorns in unity and as a community from the higher levels of the spiritual world. We are of the same energy vibration as the angelic kingdom. We too hold a vast heart, swelling with love for humanity. We are your helpers, your guides; we are here to lead you forth. Search for the bright shining light that emanates from the energy horns at our third eye; this is our beacon. When you truly believe in our energy and call on us to assist you in your life, you will feel the energy force and attraction of our beacon of light leading you forth along the correct spiritual path for you.

Each of you has a special unicorn that you can call on to assist you in your life. You can also visit the unicorn kingdom on the inner planes of the spiritual world to form a deeper connection with us, the unicorns. This can be achieved by simply asking us to transport you to our kingdom; either during your sleep state, or during meditation. We are present and offer our support, energy and wisdom to all of humanity. This is our main mission and message. We come to share the love, power and energy of the unicorn kingdom with you. Open your hearts to us now! Call us into your lives and allow our energy to surround you with a blanket of love. We are here as supportive guides for all of humanity. Please do not doubt our energies or power because we take the form of an animal. It is our appearance that symbolizes our connection with Mother Earth, the animal and elemental kingdoms. When you open to our energies we can balance, clear and activate your vibrational light body with cosmic, high vibrational light. We will deepen your connection with the beloved soul of Mother Earth and help all to see, sense and understand the light being helpers who assist Mother Earth and care for nature."

Unicorns, angels and archangels all come from the Great Spiritual Plane and are powerful spiritual healers. They heal on all vibrational levels; physical, emotional, mental and spiritual. Unicorns offer healing through Christ consciousness and white light (split into rainbow colours through prisms) while angels and archangels each work with one specific colour ray frequency to bring healing, inspiration and wholeness. Archangel Raphael works with emerald green light for healing, for example, while Archangel Zadkiel uses the violet ray light frequency in form of the Violet Flame.

The body is a physical expression of the mental being. Your body was chosen by you before you incarnated because it offered you certain learning opportunities and because you felt that it suited you. In fact, once you are in your body you are still continuously influencing the way it looks through the many lifestyle, accessory and nutrition choices you make every day. For example, you can choose to colour your hair, get tattoos, adorn your body with jewellery, draw symbols on your body using henna or other body paints, exercise excessively or not at all, eat a balanced diet or ignore your body's nutritional needs, wear extravagant make-up or go barefaced, and many other decisions in this vein.

The process of choosing a body is somewhat like going shopping for clothes. You go into a shop that has various styles, looks, and designs on offer, for different intents and purposes; and you choose the "look" that most suits you, and that you feel most comfortable with. In other words, you choose outer clothes and accessories that you feel convey a message about who you are on the inside. In the same way, you have chosen your body to express the inner you. The body is an outward projection of the mind. Your body communicates many things on the non-verbal, emotional and visual level. Linguists and psychologists agree that around eighty per cent of all communication is conveyed non-verbally through body language. Your body communicates a lot of information about you -- who you are, the thoughts you think, and the messages you send out to the world around you.

In the same way that humans consciously choose their bodies, the elemental and angelic kingdoms choose the physical forms they project as well. The unicorns have chosen the radiant white colour of their coat to convey and evoke the virtues of purity, innocence (in a spiritual sense), power, beauty and unconditional love. They choose the shape of a horse to convey their deep connection to Mother Earth and all of nature. Many humans find it easier to connect with animals than with other humans; and they find it easier to accept the unconditional love, service and devotion animals offer them. Unicorns are emanations of divine love, they are devoted to all of creation, and they evolve through service to the divine will. The unicorns also have energy horns on their forehead that signify the awakened or actualized third eye. Unicorns vibrate at very high frequencies, and work closely with the angels to assist the spiritual development of humanity.

The unicorns are a powerful and unwavering source of love. When you look into a unicorn's eyes and heart, you see the beauty of the Creator's love. It is like looking straight into the heavens, blissful and healing. The unicorns hold within their souls the ability to demonstrate to us a Divine vision of the Earth as a civilization based on love, unity and harmony, and to remind us of our own infinite capacity to love, while assisting us in gazing deep into the soul of the Creator. A unicorn's eyes and soul can act as a mirror for the divine and sacred energy within your own being, helping you to remember who you really are – a child of the Divine – and showing you the presence of heaven within you.

Many people who connect with the unicorns cry tears of joy when they first gaze into the eyes of their unicorn guide because they see reflected within themselves what they have been searching for throughout their many incarnations on Earth.

The unicorns are the mirror that allows you to gaze into the pure inner being of your soul. This is the reason why the unicorn energies are powerfully healing, inspiring and nurturing – they connect us with the God-Mind within. It is also the reason why they are linked with manifestation and magic. When you call on the unicorn energies to surround you and radiate their healing light, they send high frequencies waves of love into your being and soul but they also activate the natural healing energies within you, supporting you as healing takes place. In old myths, the unicorns are said to grant wishes to the pure of heart, but what this really means is that they teach manifestation and healing skills to those who are ready.

They function like a mirror for the Higher Self within you, reminding you of your Divine nature and activating the healing energy within you; aligning, balancing and purifying your entire being. People often say they have been healed by the unicorns but the truth is, they have healed themselves. Each of us has the inner knowledge to activate our own healing energies and connect with our true nature, the God-Mind within, but we have forgotten. In sleep and other altered states where our intellect is not the dominant vibration, we know exactly how to activate our healing energy (and we often do, which is one of the reasons why sleep is essential for physical and mental health) but when the intellect is involved it creates a shield (of doubt, scepticism, and distrust) before your healing energy, hindering its expression. The reason is that your intellect has not yet realised or placed faith in the healing source within you.

Meditation: Self-Healing

In a state of relaxation or meditation, call on your unicorn guide to join you and surround you with their love and healing light energy. Then ask to look in your guide's eyes or heart to see the truth; the sacred and healing energies within you. You can imagine this or simply acknowledge that it is happening, focusing on your feelings.

Your unicorn guide will guide you appropriately. It is important to remember that any healing energies you experience are coming from within you, as the unicorns act as mirrors to gaze into your soul. You need faith, trust and confidence in order to open up to the sacred healing energies within you and to recognize them as the source of all healing. Only you can heal yourself. Any healing given by another is always an awakening, an ignition, or an actualization of your own sacred healing energy and the infinite intelligence that is present in every cell of your body. If you do not initially receive any insights or sensations during this meditation, thank your unicorn guide for the love and healing energy given to you and rest peacefully in the knowledge that while it is not yet your time to achieve knowledge of the sacred healing power within you, once the necessary additional growth steps have been completed, realization must come.

Unicorn and Pegasus

The unicorn, which is depicted with his third eye open, is an ascended being with superior higher seeing and wisdom faculties. Unicorn people are energetically clear, high vibration beings whose third eyes are open and active. This does not necessarily mean that they are clairvoyant or psychic in the sense of being able to see vivid mental images, colour and light in other dimensions. Many people are claircogniscent -- they simply know.

Wings are an outer sign of a fully developed, or actualized, heart centre. Angel wings are an emanation of love from their heart centre. For this reason, angel and archangels are depicted with wings that extend from their body at the level of their heart chakra at the back of their torsos. A Pegasus is depicted as a flying horse with wings, also extending from the level of the heart. There are also some pictures of unicorns with wings and sometimes we meet these unicorns in our meditations. Angel or Pegasus people are those from whom light radiates like wings.

Consciously or unconsciously, they can extend their wings and fold them around people or animals, conveying a sense of peace, protection and love. The roles and healing qualities of the Unicorn and Pegasus are slightly different. The unicorn inspires, gives hope, empowers and enlightens; while the heart-centred Pegasus comforts, protects and succours.

The Vibrational Qualities of the Elemental Realm

Fairies

Fairies are very small etheric beings who manifest in all the colours of the rainbow. They are associated with the air element and look after Mother Earth's flowers and plants. Fairies are extremely powerful healers and will lovingly help humans with healing, especially with clearing very deep emotional blocks in your energy system. The fairy kingdom expresses a deep love for all humans. Collectively, they send out streams of healing energy vibrations which contain a multitude of colour ray frequencies, representing the energy of their soul and their creativity to humans who are open and receptive to receiving these energies. Open your heart to the fairy kingdom and accept the healing energy that they lovingly send you. Allow it to integrate with your being, inspiring a deeper connection with nature and new creativity and enthusiasm for life in you.

Breathe in the energy of the fairies and you will receive the vibrational essence of the fairy kingdom. Let it flow into your being and melt into your soul. Allow yourself to form a deeper connection with the fairies. Their work is still unknown and unappreciated by most of mankind. They wish for you to allow them into your life and being, honouring their presence on the Earth as well as assisting them with their task of healing and balancing the energies of Mother Earth.

The fairies are beings of pure love. They are like the unicorns and angels of the nature world, small orbs of light that gather in the countryside by flowers, plants and rivers. People very rarely see their tiny energy orbs. There are millions of fairies across the countryside and in gardens and parks battling against the after-effects of the careless and often destructive behaviour of humans and the damage it causes to the beauty, balance and harmony of nature. The fairies are eager to assist gardeners, farmers and nature conservationists and use their love and healing energy to make sure the new flowers and plants paint the world in wonderfully varied colours of beauty and light.

The fairies look after the flowers as though they are babies. They infuse them with light and support them energetically with the creation of their luscious green leaves and beautifully coloured petals. They receive intuitive guidance from Infinite Intelligence on how to balance the Earth's energies, how to care for her fruits and how to heal the parts of her body that are scarred, broken or infected by the building of roads, cities, and other manmade structures. The fairies give healing to Mother Earth to ease the stress put on her. As the guardians of the nature world and the vibrational consciousness of the more complex life within nature, they feel the pain of the plants when they are neglected or destroyed and they suffer when the high vibration healing energies of nature are blocked beneath thick layers of concrete. Have you ever wondered why you feel recharged after a day outdoors in nature, but you feel exhausted and worn out after spending a day in a busy, loud city centre or indoors with artificial lighting? It is because the healing energy of nature can flow much more freely to you in an environment where it is not suppressed or blocked. Efforts are being made to introduce more parks into cities and more plant life and "green" energy into office buildings. People are starting to wake up to the fact that they are healthier and more productive when they remain in contact with nature and her healing energies. The fairies welcome these efforts with open arms and rejoice in the slow re-awakening of humankind's connection with nature and the more subtle energies of life. Fairies inspire you to sit and walk in nature, not only so that you can connect with the fairies and nature spirits but so that you can receive the waves of energy that flow from the core of the Earth, through the soil, into the atmosphere around you and out into the universe. These waves of energy ground you, infuse you with the love of Mother Earth and provide healing life force energy to the human body and soul.

The fairies do not want you to feel guilty for their hard work in caring and protecting the nature world but they are now making themselves heard to ask you to help them. You are a physical being, which means you can absorb energy and radiate it in a physical way that will greatly benefit Mother Earth and the nature world, anchoring the healing energy.

The rainbow love energy that flows from the fairy kingdom to you is given freely. Accept their unconditional love into your energy field by imagining it melting into your aura or flowing in through your crown chakra, travelling down your chakra column and into the earth star chakra below your feet. Whenever you are in nature, near flowers or close to a tree invoke this protective, healing and loving energy of the fairies. Let them know that you wish to give healing to Mother Earth and nature in response to their request to you. You will probably feel a rush of energy through your system. Imagine, sense or know that as the energy flows through your being, you direct one beam of healing energy down into the Earth, extending deep down into the core of Mother Earth; and you radiate a second beam of light outward from your heart chakra, travelling to whichever aspect of nature you wish to heal. Whether you send your healing energy to a vegetable patch, flowers on your windowsill or a vast expanse of forest, the fairies will be grateful for all the healing energy that is anchored into the Earth through human beings. You have the power to heal the nature world and if only a handful of people practice this healing in their daily lives then the energy vibration of the Earth will raise and Mother Earth will heal her being. It is important now for humans to take responsibility for the land and the many spirit beings that exist within each plant and blade of grass.

Be forgiving of the mistakes of others and take it into your hands to do the healing work whenever you come across nature along your path. Not much time or effort is needed; if you are walking past a flower you do no not have to stop, it only requires one thought and the healing energy that is necessary will flow from your being.

You can sit in your garden and invite the fairies to join you as you send healing to the garden; or in a park; or by the beach. Any place that contains plant life is filled with the subtle energies of nature and has fairies looking after it, healing it and nurturing it. The task that the fairies ask of you is so small and takes only a few minutes of your time. Make a vow to the fairies to assist them in their healing work and you will make friends for life. The fairies are forgiving and understand that you do not always remember but they bless you with their gratitude if you make the effort to assist them and form an intention to stay in tune with the subtle energies of nature.

Elves

Elves are very high vibration beings and extremely powerful magical healers. They are experts in crystal healing and will lovingly teach you their wisdom and assist with your healing, reconnecting you to your true self and your conscious union with All-That-Is. Elves are associated with earth energy. Working with the elves, fauns, gnomes, and other earth energies is essential in these times of pollution and environmental damage. Reconnecting with earth energy gives you a renewed sense of who you are, and your purpose in life. Earth energy is associated with growth, beauty, fertility, nurture, and stability. Gods and Goddesses associated with earth energy are Gaia, Hecate, Cerridwen, Isis, Freya, Geb and Osiris. Earth spirits have a special connection with Archangel Uriel. People born under an earth sign – Taurus, Virgo, or Capricorn – are great lovers of beauty and luxury in all areas of life; they are usually gourmets who enjoy good food, and love decorating their home to suit their tastes. They usually feel great affinity with creatures of earth, such as dogs, cows, bears, moles and badgers. Earth crystals include aventurine, malachite, obsidian, and fossils.

Gnomes

Gnomes are nature spirits of the earth. They help look after Mother Earth's soil, keeping it in balance and nourished, so that the planet keeps its physical equilibrium and we have a place to grow and evolve.

Fauns

Fauns are nature beings that have the appearance of half human, half goat. The Nature God Pan looks like a Faun, but is much taller. Fauns are dedicated to helping Mother Earth's trees.

Dryads (Tree Spirits or Tree People)

Trees have a long tradition of association with spirituality, magic and healing. The ancient Celtic druids are known as the "people of the tree knowledge". They derived much of their wisdom from the oak trees. Their Rune Stone system is said to be based upon symbols they received from tress and they held their ceremonies in groves. Many trees were considered sacred or revered for their medicinal properties, including the pine, olive, laurel, and willow. In fact, white willow bark is the original source of aspirin (acetylsalicylacid) and was used for its painkilling, anti-inflammatory properties for millennia before modern science learned about its benefits.

Tree spirits are the soul, or life force energy, of each tree. Each tree spirit is unique, and has a different personality, complete with quirks and personal tastes and preferences. Connecting with the life force energy of a tree is very rewarding, and you can learn a lot from a tree spirit (just like the druids did). Hippies are sometimes laughingly referred to as "tree huggers" but hugging a tree and absorbing some of its healing life force energy is actually a very healthy thing to do.

Nature Spirits

Everything in nature is animated by Spirit and is an emanation of the One substance. Just as each tree has a spirit so does each plant. Successful gardeners accept and honour these plant spirits. You can communicate (silently or out loud) with the spirit of a plant and it will let you know what it needs. Trust your intuition. You may hear or feel that the plant needs shielding from harsh sunlight, or it may ask for more water. Be intuitive – and you will work in partnership with the fairies and see remarkable results!

Sylphs

Sylphs are beautiful nature spirits of air. The word "sylph" comes from the Greek "sylphe", meaning butterfly. It is no coincidence that fairies are often depicted with butterfly wings. They feel a great affinity to these air spirits. Sylphs are free spirits who like to dance and ride the currents of the air. They are drawn to movement, rhythm, energy, innocence, creativity and enthusiasm. Poetry, stories and music, especially sung or played on string or wind instruments like the harp appeal greatly to them. They can be quite tall and human in appearance although they can change shape. They are very high vibration beings and like to help humans by providing you with inspiration, especially in creative projects. Ancient myths contain many incidences of air gods giving the gift of life, via the breath, to humankind. Adam, the "man of the earth", was animated and given life by God's breath. In Norse mythology, the God Odin blew Ond (the breath of life) into two trees and by this action created the first man and woman. Chi or Qi, the name of the life force in Chinese philosophy, is said to be the breath of the Cosmic Dragon. The word "spirit" itself translates to "breath", derived from the Latin "spiro", meaning "I breathe". Meditation often uses focus on the breath to connect the mind and the body in our awareness. Air energy is associated with ideas, logic, messages, visualization, communication, adaptability, new horizons, freedom, knowledge, travel, and the search for truth. Air spirits are the messengers of the natural world, often working together with angels. Air elementals communicate messages via thoughts, dreams and the music of the wind. *Zephyrs* are another form of air spirits. People born under the influence of an air sign – Aquarius, Gemini, or Libra – are good communicators, quick and creative thinkers, and usually feel great affection for animals that fly in the air, such as eagles, owls, and butterflies. Air spirits have a special connection with Archangel Raphael. Gods and Goddesses associated with air energy include Artemis/ Diana, Athena, Parvati, Psyche, Hermes, Mercury, Jupiter, Horus and Odin. Air crystals are citrine, clear quartz, and amethyst.

Salamanders

Salamanders are nature spirits of fire and the small cousins of dragons. They are associated with fire energy and its manifestations such as lightning, electricity and sunlight. Connecting with fire energy can bring creativity, courage, transformation and positive action into your life. People who were born under a fire sign – Aries, Leo, or Sagittarius -- are usually creative, charismatic and strong-willed. They usually feel a strong affinity for "fiery" or "fierce", stinging or otherwise powerful animals such as lions, tigers, lizards, bees, dragonflies and stags. Archangel Michael is associated with fire energy. Using candles indoors in a controlled environment is an effective and safe way to work with fire magic. Gods and Goddesses associated with fire energy include Brighid, Kali, Pele, Sekhmet, Medusa, Vesta, Apollo, Lugh, and Ra. Fire crystals are amber, garnet, bloodstone, sunstone and jasper.

Mermaids and Mermen

Mermaids and Mermen are spirits of water. They can be rather tall and shape shift into human appearance. They hold much wisdom and are wonderful healers. Water energy is associated with psychic and healing abilities, the subconscious and dream work, as well as emotions. The principle of water is love. Mermaids and Mermen can also incarnate in human bodies for soul development. Human mermaids and mermen usually have long flowing hair, a great affinity with water which shows in a strong attraction to oceans, lakes, and rivers, and a love of water animals such as dolphins, sea turtles, and seahorses. Incarnated mermaids and mermen are often born under a water sign as Pisces, Cancer or Scorpio. Gods and Goddesses associated with the water energy include Aphrodite, Morrigan, Coventina, Poseidon/ Neptune, Tlaloc, and all goddesses of sacred wells and springs. Water spirits have a special connection with Archangel Gabriel. Water crystals include moonstone, pearl, and aquamarine.

Undines

Undines, the Greek term for "sea sprites", are nature spirits of water. They are colourful and shimmery in appearance, reminiscent of fish's scales. They are small in size and help to look after Mother Earth's oceans and lakes.

<u>The Fifth Element: Spirit</u>

When all the elements are working together in harmony, you sense the fifth element, which is pure Spirit, *akasa*, substance or ether. It is the element or substance of the divine and the matter of which the manifest universe is made. As you work with the four elements, you will begin to sense Spirit as the spiral, vortex or matrix of energy which permeates and transcends all life. You may also begin to sense and meet the elemental beings!

Are Mythological Creatures Real?

People often ask me if the nature spirits and other mythological creatures are real, and if they truly exist; or if they are just imaginary beings from folklore, legend and mythology. My response is that they are just as real as you are. Quantum physics and mystical meditation show us that there is only one absolute reality – the All, or the first cause; that is the infinite intelligence or the creative force of the universe; omnipresent, omnipotent and omniscient. The Absolute manifests itself vibrationally in many forms, many worlds, and many dimensions of consciousness. First there is Mind, then Matter – which is a form of Mind at slower vibrational rates making for denser energy. Matter feels real to us because we can see, hear, touch, smell and taste it. If we had different sense awareness organs, we would experience very different realities. A tick for example has a physical sense awareness that is finely tuned to perceive two specific things: the smell of butter acid (sweat) and a certain degree of warmth (body temperature). Its senses are exclusively tuned into these two factors because it survives by sucking the blood of warm blooded animals, including humans. It sits in wait, on a branch in the forest, and when the perfect conditions arise (a human or animal passing beneath the tree) and are conveyed through the senses, it jumps. Obviously, to us the tick's world view is incredibly limited but from the point of view of the higher dimensions, the human body is equally limited. Our physical sense awareness is finely tuned to enable us to survive in a material three-dimensional environment. This has advantages, because it allows us to focus on the important things and block out superfluous information – imagine hearing all radio channel frequencies simultaneously for instance! But we have to be aware of our physical limitations. William Blake, the poet, said, "When we see with, and not through the eye, we are fooled". So, do not always believe your senses. For example, the ground you are sitting or lying on right now while reading this book may seem stationary, but it is not – the planet is spinning at around 1670 kilometres per hour!

To say we don't believe something because we can't see it is getting the wrong end of the stick – it is more likely that we can't see it because we don't believe it. The "observer theory" in quantum physics has proven that an observer is a necessary requirement for anything to exist at all. In other words, if a tree falls in the wood and there is nobody around to hear it, it does *not* make a sound. Also, objects behave differently when they are viewed. We live in a universe that physical science does not yet fully understand. Mental science (meditation) opens us to higher dimensions and allows us to transcend the limitations of a three-dimensional awareness. According to the Hermetic principle, "as above, so below", we find that within our minds we hold the keys to understanding the greater reality of the universe and the answers to all questions. The higher most God and the innermost God are one God.

Everything in the manifest and unmanifest universe is animated, sustained and enfolded in God, or infinite intelligence. Everything vibrates. Everything is consciousness, mind, or intelligence. Bodies are formed as outformings or "clothes" for vibrational consciousness. Therefore, every part of the manifested universe (matter) has a consciousness that animates it and this consciousness projects itself into a physical body. Matter is energy so the physical bodies of entities will be denser or more subtle depending on the vibration of the energy but it is still a physical body for a mental, spiritual, conscious being. Many elemental or spiritual beings can change their bodies and their appearance at will; because they are more in touch with the creative forces of their own mind, and the way the mind controls physicality. This is called shape shifting, and it is something that human souls can do in the inter-life (the life between lives) when the etheric body is far more subtle.

My near death experience and my communications with the unicorns have taught me many things about the life after death, also known as the interlife (the life between lives), which I will talk about in the next chapter. I will also discuss how the unicorns use past life regression as a healing tool.

CHAPTER 11

Understanding Past Lives and Their Relevance

> *"For we know that if our earthly house of this tabernacle were dissolved, we have a building of God, a house not made with hands, eternal in the heavens."*
> *- 2 Corinthians (5:1)*

The Rhythm of Life

A human life moves from the moment of conception to birth, the lifespan and finally physical death. As such it can be seen to move between the two poles of "birth" and "death". In a physical sense this is correct because as humans we perceive time as moving forward in a linear motion and we see that the body, which is formed during pregnancy and individuated in birth, matures, grows older and finally "dies" and decomposes, entering back into the material cycle of life ("dust to dust"). This cycle of germination, generation, degeneration, and decomposition of the physical body is a classic example of the "rise and fall", the "ebb and flow", the rhythm that is characteristic of all life. This steady movement occurs along the poles within the physical, mental and spiritual planes. The hermetic text *The Kybalion* explains the Principle of Rhythm with the words: "Everything flows, out and in; everything has its tides; all things rise and fall; the pendulum swing manifests in everything; the measure of the swing to the right is the measure of the swing to the left; rhythm compensates".

Suns, worlds, humans, animals, plants, minerals, forces, energy, mind, matter, all that exist manifest this principle. Rhythm manifests in the creation and destruction of worlds, in the rise and fall of cultures, and in the mental states of humans. This rhythm is reflected in the motion of your breath. Mystics say that universes begin and end with the exhaling and inhaling of The All, or God. Universes are created, reach their extreme point of materiality, and then begin their upward swing or ascent toward Mind, or Consciousness. Suns are created from gases, reach their maximum point of density and finally burn out turning back into energy and the building blocks for new creations. All the suns and worlds are born, grow, die only to be reborn. The same holds true for individuated consciousness in a physical body. In the course of your soul development you project yourself into physicality (the outward breath) in different bodies, circumstances, and experiences and as your understanding grows, you start the inner journey to God consciousness (the inward breath).

How to "Rise Above It"

Knowing about the Principle of Rhythm helps you understand and transmute the bewildering succession of moods, feelings, and other annoying and confusing changes that you notice in yourself and others. There are two general planes of consciousness: the lower and the higher. When you are conscious of the effect that the Principle of Rhythm has on your mental state, you can use this awareness to, quite literally, rise above it. You can consciously rise to the higher plane of consciousness and escape the rhythmic ebb and flow on the lower plane. Without this conscious awareness, the rhythmic "pendulum swing" of moods and emotions rules your life and you often don't even know why you feel the way you feel. Often, periods of enthusiasm are invariably followed by feelings of depression, or relationship harmony is followed by discord and arguments. Perhaps you have never considered that your moods and emotions rise and fall like the tides of the sea according to a natural law. Realizing this, you can refuse to let your moods and negative mental states affect you.

This enables you to know yourself better and allows you to remain in touch with your authentic self at all times. The law always operates meaning that the pendulum always swings (your biological rhythm and the corresponding moods that manifest always fluctuate), but by applying your awareness to it you can avoid being carried along with it.

In this way, you transform your daily life into a spiritual practice.

Unicorns and Past Life Recalls

The unicorns, as emanations of divine love, assure us that nothing is ever forgotten: *"Every experience is important. Every moment you live adds to the Beingness of All-That-Is. Every breath you breathe expands the Allness of The All. On a personal level, every experience you have, whether you view it as "good", "bad" or "neutral" at the time is a learning experience for your soul. Nothing is ever wasted."*

The unicorns have also explained to me that *karma* does not work as punishment but rather as an opportunity for growth and an expansion of understanding. For example, if you are very cruel and self-centred in one lifetime, you may choose to come back in a position of servitude or dependency in which you can experience the effects of cruelty first-hand. In the interlife, the life between lives that you spend in non-physicality, you – the individuated stream of consciousness that is You – always understands the bigger picture and is given a lot of help, teaching and advice by advanced, or ascended, beings in order to progress spiritually. There is no judgement apart from the judgement you place on yourself.

The unlimited love of God places no blame, distributes no punishments and makes no distinctions between right and wrong. Every life experience is cherished because it adds to the development of the whole. Even intensely negative experiences such as the Holocaust for example, are transmuted and healed on the higher levels.

The unicorns say to me: *"It is not very helpful to know your past lives simply for curiosity's sake. Many people make the mistake to explore their past lives like a 'spiritual tourist', getting lost in the exciting details and everyday scenarios just as they did the first time around [when they were actually living those lives]. If you wish to explore your past lives, it is beneficial to use your intuition as a guide on issues that warrant healing. Utilized like this, past life regression can be a useful tool for healing and self-growth."*

I discovered the healing power of "targeted" regression (regression that targets a specific issue or problem) for myself during a deep trance state. From my early teenage years, for almost two decades, I suffered from continuous throat infections that were so severe that I had to regularly take strong antibiotics, as my (in all other aspects healthy) body fought with raging fevers and seemed unable to ward off these infections on its own. When I was fifteen, I missed several weeks of school due to persistent bronchitis and in my early twenties, while studying medicine at university in Cologne in Germany I once took an important written exam with a high grade 41C [105.8 F] fever and unable to speak because of a serious throat infection. I went to a doctor later that same day who diagnosed me with a triple infection of bronchitis, tonsillitis and scarlet fever. I always felt there was a deeper cause for my persistent, recurrent throat problems and often asked my inner guide about it. As I learned different spiritual healing techniques, I focussed on my throat area, clearing any accumulated karma or energy blockages in the throat chakra. I noticed an improvement but I still had throat infections every winter and, remarkably, they often seemed to be accompanied by a complete loss of voice for two or three days. After my brain tumour experience had given me a crash course in mental and spiritual healing through positive thinking, affirmations, visualizations and spiritual mind treatment, I decided that enough was enough and I was ready to get to the bottom of my throat problems. I carried this intention with me, until one day during my pregnancy with Elias, while lying on my sofa listening to a self-hypnosis course for relaxation and childbirth preparation, I fell into a deep trance state and suddenly felt somebody choking or strangling me from behind. Their grip was iron-hard around my throat and they were squeezing so tightly I couldn't breathe. The sensation was so vivid that I was petrified with fear, trembling and shaking, unable to move. I felt the insides of my throat burning. I was mute, silent, unable to break free and fight for my life. The experience lasted for about one or two minutes and it was as real to me as the sofa I was lying on, as though there really was somebody in my living room, strangling me from behind, squeezing the life force out of me and sentencing me to silence and death. Suddenly I realized, *This is what happened to me. They killed me because they did not like what I was saying. I am afraid to speak out about spiritual truths as a result of what happened to me in another lifetime. My throat problems are a result of this persecution and death through strangulation. Any negative emotion I feel gets focussed and expressed in the throat area because the memory of this event is so strong.* As soon as I gave voice to this realization, the feeling of strangulation stopped. The sensation was over, but the feeling and the insight stayed with me. This was two years ago and I have not had a single throat infection since. My intuition tells me that I was strangulated at the stake (or in another public place) because the religious establishment of the time saw me as an uncomfortable trouble maker. They painted me as a witch and killed me to silence me because I was sharing spiritual truths derived from meditation and mystical experiences, which did not conform to the dogma of the official church teachings. I was empowering people to think for themselves and discover their own truth, within themselves, and this was seen as an antagonistic force by those in power who wanted to keep people's minds and bodies enslaved and controlled by dogma, social hierarchy and fear.

In this life, I have not felt comfortable sharing my spiritual journey with many people until recently. I was fiercely independent in my spiritual studies and only trusted a select few people with my spiritual insights, practices and discoveries. Part of my hesitation to be openly spiritual was worry about my academic reputation and career, but on a deeper level I was petrified of "revealing" myself as a mystic or spiritual seeker because it (irrationally, but very real to me) did not feel safe. I felt vulnerable and "bare" in my spiritual nature, and was fiercely protective about my spiritual practices, including meditation and communication with higher beings. I now realize, due to the spontaneous past life recall, that I associated spirituality (particularly mysticism and a personal quest for truth as opposed to passively accepting the prevalent religious dogma of the day) with vulnerability, prosecution and alienation. Since I have healed this past-life aspect of myself, I am much freer in discussing my spirituality and with the help and inspiration of the unicorns, I am becoming more outspoken and authentic every day. I am learning to consistently act and think from my higher self without feelings of doubt, confusion, or uncertainty – which are all derivations of fear – clouding my mind. The feeling of vulnerability and fear in regards to lived spirituality has completely vanished after the past-life aspect revealed itself and was understood, accepted, integrated and healed.

The Principle of Polarity

Everything in this universe is manifested along two poles. Heat and cold, love and hate, light and darkness are not really opposites but variations of degree. Opposites are identical in nature but different in degree. All manifested things have to aspects, sides, or poles. Likewise, Spirit and matter are two extremes of the same things, with many intermediate planes (variances in degree, or vibration) between them. Looking at a thermometer, there is no place that you could point to and say, "This is where cold ends and warm begins." It is all a matter of higher or lower vibrations. High and low are relative terms themselves, the two being poles of the same thing and only gaining meaning when viewed in comparison to another point on the scale.

What this means is that you can transmute one end of the pole into the other. By raising your vibration, you can transform hatred into love, darkness into light, and negativity into positivity. The positive pole is of a higher vibration than the negative and is the dominating force. Nature always tends towards the dominant activity of the positive pole. If you do not think any thoughts, you are in your natural state, which is happiness. Your true, unadulterated nature is positivity. Nature will always assist you in moving upwards along the poles when transforming your vibrations.

5 Tools to Connect with the Unicorns for Past Life Healing

By healing unresolved aspects of our past lives, we become more aware, productive and loving. The unicorns wish to be of service with the healing of past life trauma because once we have integrated neglected aspects of ourselves it becomes easier to raise our vibrations to connect with the unicorns and angelic kingdoms. The most important factor is to set your intention. Ask the unicorns for help with healing past-life residues, energies or complexes that are holding you back from expressing your full potential in this life.

The following tools will help you to connect with the unicorns for the purpose of past life healing:

(1) Dreams

Before you fall asleep, think about the issue you are requesting healing for. Hold it in your mind's eye and affirm, *"I realize that some mistakes (errors in thinking) have been made in this situation. I kindly ask for the assistance of the unicorns with healing this aspect of myself. May all errors and their effects be undone in all directions of time."* Pay particular attention to your dreams that night. It is a good idea to have a dream diary in which you can write down any dreams and messages from the unicorns. Remember, the unicorns often communicate in the form of vivid picture sequences or movies and they often use symbolical meanings in order to impart deeper truths (such as the image of the fish in my "pearl meditation" symbolizing my true self).

(2) Scents

Unicorns are like finely tuned instruments. Their sense awareness is highly developed. Remember, you don't see because you have eyes, you have eyes because you see. You don't hear because you have ears, you have ears because you hear. Sense awareness is an act of consciousness. The physical organs are merely tools that facilitate the mental perception in this three dimensional time-space reality. As consciousness vibrates to a higher and higher rate, so do the sense awarenesses. Unicorns have a highly evolved sense of smell. They love the smell of happiness and hate the stench of anger. They are drawn to the sublime scent of love and are repulsed by the rotten, decomposing smell of hate. You can use incense, essential oils and flower essences to connect with the unicorn vibrations and invite them to join you in meditation with the purpose of past life healing.

(3) Music

Just as they have a highly evolved sense of smell, the unicorns can hear notes and tones that are out of our range such as the melodies emitted by growing flowers, as well as the colours of their blossoms. Every living thing sends out music, whether it is flowers growing, the sun rising or a planet moving. You aura also plays musical notes, the quality and sound of which depends on the state of it. Your unicorn can hear it all. A colourful garden full of flowers, a vibrant lawn and a water fountain emanates wonderful musical notes, which is healing for the planet. To a unicorn, it sounds like an orchestra playing a beautiful symphony. An unkempt garden full of litter and a stagnant lifeless pond sounds like discordant, harsh and jagging music to your unicorn. The unicorns can hear the music of the spheres, the melody of running water, the sigh of the wind and the angels singing. As its hearing is so sensitive it is very difficult for a unicorn to be near the hum of an electric pylon and they find the discord of quarrelling, screaming or any form of aggressiveness very uncomfortable, including discordant emotions, whether acted or real, emitting from TV and radio. Emotions have a sound and a smell. Anger sounds like a bark and has an acidic scent, jealousy sounds like a growl and smells of ammonia whereas love, joy and compassion sound like angelic hymns. Love smells like the delicate perfume scent of a fragrant rose and compassion like a lily. There are many vibrations of sound and smell (as well as other sense awarenesses) taking place all around us without us noticing. Your unicorn's own pure and beautiful aura plays the most exquisite melodies and harmonics, far above your auditory range. It is so glorious that it tunes everything around it up to a higher octave. The sounds the unicorns emit can touch people profoundly, in the very depths of their souls.

Unicorns hear and respond to the intention of sounds and music, so listen to beautiful elevating music, sacred chants, choirs singing in harmony (gospel, medieval, classic) to raise your vibrations and attract the unicorns to you to work with you on past life issues and healing.

(4) Candles

Candles represent light, outer light as well as the mystic inner light. Humans are discovering that as they raise their vibrations, they can see subtle shades that they could not see before, including the energy and colour of auras. More and more people are opening up to spiritual development and are developing their psychic vision (clairvoyance and claircogniscence) in the process. Unicorns are fully enlightened, all seeing, all knowing beings, so they can see a spectrum way beyond our visual range. Unicorns see with both their physical eyes and their third eye.

To use a candle to connect with your unicorn with the purpose of past life healing, place a candle in front of you, taking care that it is safe. You may wish to choose a white candle to represent the unicorn energy. If you are strongly drawn towards a different colour, it may be that a particular Archangel or Ascended Master wishes to assist your unicorn with the past life healing process, so go with your intuition at all times. Gaze into the candle flame for a few minutes. Feel your eyes closing regularly. It will become more difficult to open them and eventually, you will feel like resting your eye lids. Close your eyes. At this point, the image of the candle flame will flicker in your mind's eye, behind your forehead. Concentrate your awareness on this light. Feel it expand until there is nothing in your perception apart from this light. Meditate on the inner light. Your unicorn will join you in meditation when you call it and work with you on any issues or blockages that you wish to clear and heal.

(5) Crystals

Crystals have a consciousness and energy that can be harnessed and used. You can take any one of the five "unicorn jewels" (clear quartz, rose quartz, jelly opal, selenite or pearl) and cleanse, charge and dedicate it to your work with the unicorn energy. There are many ways to cleanse a crystal: chanting the scared Om over it, washing it in clear water, placing it in sunlight, playing a singing bowl over it, or blowing on it. You can charge it with chanting, by leaving it out in the moonlight, or placing it in fast flowing water or another high energy spot. Most important is the setting of your intention. You may want to place the crystal on your third eye while dedicating it to past-life healing work with the unicorns. You can then carry your crystal around with you, meditate with it, or place it on your unicorn altar or power spot. It will work with you on an energetic level to bring about your request.

Exploring Infinity

Our incarnations are our "road home". Every time you incarnate, you learn, grow and evolve, always drawing closer to the Creator by uncovering who-you-really-are, an emanation of the divine. The physical body is a finite vehicle for the infinite passenger inside it. Jesus said, "the body is the temple of the soul". Life is a school, a growth process. It is a school run by the most benevolent, unconditionally loving teacher. There are no exams and you cannot fail. It does not matter if you are slow or quick to learn, because you have an eternity to absolve your lessons. Every soul is successful in returning home, because every soul is an emanation of Divine Mind, and Divine Mind is *always* successful.

Goethe, the German poet, playwright, philosopher and scientist (1749 – 1832) said: "If you want to advance into the Infinite, explore the finite in all directions." This is why we choose physical incarnations. We realize the enormous potential for growth that the finite offers us. We advance into the Infinite by exploring and exercising the physical, energetic, social, emotional, cognitive-intellectual and spiritual aspects of being in all directions within the dimensions of time and space.

CHAPTER 12

Immortality

For death is no more than a turning of us over from time to
eternity.
- William Penn

Who Are You, Really?

The unicorns are eternal beings who have permanently awakened to their union with God. They are forever connected with the Divine Mind and all their actions, words and thoughts reflect the nature, will and infinite love of the Divine. In other words, they are always living from their God-Mind or Higher Self. To live is to evolve and since there is never an end, or death, of consciousness, unicorns (like us) are eternally evolving and expanding in consciousness. Unicorns, having fully actualized their God-Consciousness within, do not create karma anymore; they evolve through service to the Divine will. Their soul purpose, and their way of expressing Divine love, is to give hope and faith, to inspire and enlighten. As members of the angelic kingdom, they are beyond the need for incarnating physically, but they project a physical form that expresses their Inner Being in order to communicate with humans. Unicorns have chosen their physical form to express inner qualities, in the same way that every individual consciousness chooses their own body. They show themselves visually as white in colour to communicate purity and innocence; in the shape of a horse to symbolize strength, service and endurance; and with a horn on the forehead to indicate the awakened third eye. The unicorns represent a stage in the evolution of consciousness which humans, for the most part, have not yet attained. The unicorns are coming to this planet at this time to assist us with reaching the next step in evolution and together make the quantum leap into union consciousness.

Jesus said, "In my Father's house are many mansions". (John 14:2 KJV) The Father's house is the Divine Matrix or Infinite Mind of the Universe. The phrase "many mansions" refers to many planes of consciousness, or dimensions. Since everything, including matter is ultimately energy, or consciousness; it is different rates of vibration or frequency that determine which plane of consciousness, or which dimension, you experience. We know that the four different brain wave frequencies of the human mind create vastly different states of consciousness. This is an example of how wave frequencies and states of consciousness are mutually dependent. Matter vibrates at much denser frequencies than consciousness but the difference is one of degree, not of fundamental quality. While it is true that your soul, or God-Mind, inhibits a physical body on this material plane, it will certainly not need a physical body on a non-physical plane. Earth is a school for the soul. You chose to come here from your natural non-physical state in order to experience physicality and to utilize your five sense awarenesses to have a great variety of experiences in a material world, with the aim of broadening your perspective, evolving in consciousness and contributing to the ever expanding Beingness of All-That-Is.

When you chose to come back into the physical plane, you retained a connection with the broader non-physical part of you; the part of you that is still in non-physical form and is expanding with every experience, thought, and choice that is inspired by your physical vantage point. This broader non-physical part of you is the soul, God-Mind, Higher Self, or Inner Being within you. The broader non-physical part of you, your Higher Self, is connected with the physical expression of you via the emotional guidance system. Any thought, decision, choice, judgement, or idea that does not feel good to you is not in harmony with the perspective of your Higher Self, the broader non-physical part of you that is a perfect expression or extension of Divine Mind, always. In other words, you have a direct line into the Mind of God via the God-Mind or Higher Self within, which is the broader non-physical part of you.

You are always intrinsically connected to God. There is no way for you to be separate from God, because *nothing* is outside of God. God can only create with the one universal substance available – Itself. That is why any thought of Separation is an illusion. You can consciously separate yourself from who-you-really-are – your broader non-physical perspective, which is God or Divine Mind expressing Itself *as you* – but as you do so, you will part with authenticity, you will be denying your true self, and the result is that you feel less than good. The broader non-physical part of you, which is an expression or extension of God, always feels good; always feels alive, creative, joyful, peaceful, harmonious, prosperous, free, fulfilled, on purpose, and infinitely loving. Happiness is your natural state. When you submit to the illusion of Separation through conditioned, limited and negative thinking, or mistaken beliefs about yourself then you feel the absence of happiness, which is really the absence of (your connection with) your broader non-physical perspective or True Self.

As Ernest Holmes explains, "We are born of Eternal Day – and the Spiritual Sun shall never set upon the glory of our being, for it is the coming forth of God into self-expression."[43] God loves every one of us unconditionally, because every one of us is a self-expression of God. There are no good people or bad people in the eyes of that Absolute Consciousness which knows only perfection. We are all children of God, regardless of outer appearances or levels of soul development, as the Bible explains: "That ye may be sons of your Father who is in heaven: for he maketh his sun to rise on the evil and the good, and sendeth rain on the just and the unjust". (Matthew 5:45 ASV) Jesus said to the thief who passed from this physical plane by his side: "Today shalt thou be with me in paradise". (Luke 23:43) Immortality is a principle in nature and is our very essence, common to all of us. It is not something we purchase or gain as a reward for "good behaviour", nor is it a bargain we make with the universe.

Kitty Bishop, Ph.D.

The Unicorns' Teachings on Immortality

I first learned about the ultimate reality of life through meditation and then later, in December 2006, had all my insights confirmed during my near-death experience. The unicorns have suggested to me that the fear of death is the root of all human fears. If we can understand that death is no cause for fear, but is an occasion of growth, transmutation and expansion, we would all be free to express ourselves fully and fearlessly in our physical lives. The unicorns have asked me to communicate the following message to my fellow humans, stressing the importance of focussing on the feeling of being *alive* because, as they say:

"In all of eternity there is never a time when you are not alive, growing and thriving. There is no end to life. You always expand and evolve. The physical body dies, but with this "death" comes an incredible expansion of a now "liberated" consciousness which is free from the constraints, restrictions and limitations of a physical body. From your broader non-physical perspective you understand the nature of ultimate reality perfectly. You know the benefits of incarnation for soul development and you choose it joyfully and eagerly. You know that you never truly die, you merely transform from one form (physical) into another (non-physical). You are not your body. Your body is merely a shell, a house, a temple for the divine, eternal, consciousness-beingness that you are. Your soul chose this body as a physical vehicle to further its own growth in consciousness and to contribute to the continuous evolvement and expansion of All-That-Is. It is only tenuously connected to your body and is really independent of it at all times. This body is only its physical organ or tool of expression. It is the body that dies, and not the soul. All matter is finite, whereas consciousness is infinite. You are a spiritual being functioning on this physical plane, but transcendent of it. You are a multi- dimensional being operating in, but not restricted to, a three-dimensional world."

Your soul is immortal. As the unicorns say, there is never a time when you are not alive. Immortality really means that you continue to live after you have left this world, keeping a full memory of the self and with the continued ability to recognize your environment, to know and be known. You continue to see and be seen, to understand and be understood; in other words, you continue to be a conscious being. You retain an intact memory because remembrance is the link that binds the sequence of your lives together in a stream of continuity. Evolution and soul progression rely on memory. Memory gives meaning to experience. Real immortality is the continuance and ongoingness of the individual life, forever expanding.

The unicorns have explained to me that the physical body is finite because nature in her wisdom realizes that if you stay anywhere for too long, you would become too set, too rigid, too inflexible. Infinite wisdom ensures that you are allowed to stay just long enough to gather all the data and experience you need for the progression and evolution of your soul. You knew this before you chose to enter into physicality and you saw the wisdom and benefit of it. You knew that the change was required in order for you to advance. The unicorns also have a comforting message for us about reunion with our loved ones after (physical) death:

"It is natural for humans to miss those loved ones who have left this physical reality. You love them and cannot help missing them. But a true realization of immortality and a continuity of the individual soul or stream of consciousness will mean that your grief is not consumed by hopelessness. You will know that you have not lost your loved ones. They have merely gone before you. They are still alive as individuated consciousness and you will meet them again."

Eternity is a continuous unfoldment of time, forever expanding until time as we now experience it ceases to be. With this understanding, you see everyone you meet as "a budding genius, a becoming God, an unfolding soul, an eternal destiny".[44] Every person is an incarnation of eternity, a manifestation of the Infinite, a physically focussed limitless consciousness.

The unicorns remind us: "You do not have to wait until the time of your transitioning to meet your Creator. You meet God every moment of every day; in the soft rustling of autumn leaves, in the joyful leap of a dolphin, in the laughter of a child, in the perfect geometry of a snowflake, in the joy of friendship and love, and in the silence of your mind."

Kitty Bishop, Ph.D.

What is Life?

Life is the manifestation of the life force energy of God, individualized in you as an individual entity, because God is All-in-All. You live, move and have your being in God. You are a part of God, an individualized expression of universal consciousness. In *The Science of Mind*, Ernest Holmes writes, "That which we call *our* subjective mind is but a point in the Universal Mind where our personality maintains its individualized expression of Spirit."[45]

You are alive to give form to the formless, so that God may be more adequately and abundantly expressed. The process of the creative expression of the Infinite is never complete. You are standing at the leading edge of creation; thinking thoughts that have not yet been thought, creating what has not yet been created, living what has not yet been lived. Your life, your very Beingness, is making known the unknown, revealing the hidden, giving form to the formless.

What is Death?

Death is going beyond this three-dimensional world, the physical plane of the planet Earth, into other worlds of varying dimensions – into an ever-expanding Universe with ever-broadening horizons. There is no death. The physical body is left behind but once it is vacated, it is no longer you. You are the stream of consciousness that inhabited that physical vessel for a short time. Your life on the three-dimensional earth plane continues only as long as the body retains sufficient channels for the life force energy of Infinite Intelligence to flow through it. When these channels stop working properly, the body dies. It is like discarding old clothes. In fact, it feels like dropping an excess amount of weight. During my near-death-experience I felt incredibly light, weightless and free. Coming back into physical form felt like I was an expansive, weightless awareness, which was being forcefully shoved and squeezed into much too small, constrictive, very dense, heavy and cumbersome clothing. It was like forcing the giant genie inside the lamp in the tale of *Aladdin*.

In 1 Corinthians 15:40, the Bible says: "There are celestial bodies and bodies terrestrial: but the glory of the celestial is one, and the glory of the terrestrial is another." Birth and death are two sides of the same coin. Just as an individual soul needs to pass through the process of birth in order to experience three-dimensional life on this plane, so does the death process have the exact same purpose: To experience greater life. Where do you go when your body dies? You stay where you are but because the limitations of three-dimensional reality and physical sense awareness fall away, you experience yourself in a world of many more dimensions. Your consciousness continues to expand in direct relation to the ever-expanding Universe, with its ever-widening horizons, as it unfolds in you and about you.

Just as an unborn baby in utero cannot perceive that its world is within and part of the three-dimensional world, so it seems that we cannot perceive that our world is part of, and also within, other worlds of countless dimensions beyond this one.

Death is not a lonely experience. You are never alone because you are always in God, but beyond the everlasting presence of God you are also met by a "welcoming committee" of spirit guides, angels, relatives or other familiar figures upon your entry into non-physical – just as a baby is greeted earthside by its new relatives, loved ones and friends.

One Eternal Life

Consciousness is the only reality. Your Inner Being, which is the Infinite Intelligence of God in you as you, will always clothe you in forms that are suitable for the conditions and needs of whatever dimensional world you may be living in. Ernest Holmes wrote, "the inner man is constantly forming matter into the shape of a body; all of these evidences should prove to us that we are not going to attain immortality, but that *we are now immortal*! Our contention is not that dead men live again, but that a living man never dies".[46]

The *Bhagavad Gita* expresses the immortality of the spirit in *The Song Celestial*:

> *Never the spirit was born;*
> *The spirit shall cease to be never.*
> *Never was time it was not;*
> *End and Beginning are dreams.*

Birthless and deathless and changeless
Remaineth the spirit forever:
Death has not touched it at all,
Dead though the house of it seems.
Nay, but as when one who layeth
His worn-out robes away,
And taking new ones sayeth,
"These will I wear to-day",
So putteth by the spirit
Lightly, the garb of flesh,
And passeth to inherit
A residence afresh.47

Mysticism and the Awakened Mind

The ancient philosopher Philolaus wrote: "As for the nature and harmony, the situation is as follows. The real essence of actual things is eternal, and thus nature must partake of divine rather than of merely human intelligence. For it would be impossible for us to recognize any existing thing, unless each of the things of which the universe is composed had a real essence: this holds both for which is limiting and for what is limited."

The unicorns have taught me about the value of silence to get in touch with my true self. They say: *"You can discover the great truth of oneness, interconnectedness, and eternity in the silence of your own mind. When the lips are closed, there is room for the heart to speak. When the heart is silent, the great inner mystery of the soul can blaze up and illuminate life."*

By following their advice I have discovered that this is the secret that all the mystics know. The practice of silence is the key to inner wisdom. The unicorns have given me the following instructions on how to use the practice of silence to come in contact with the inner light:

"You walk the inner path by stopping all external activity, disengaging your physical senses from the world around you, and moving into silence. Silence is deepened by sitting and bringing attention to the breath. You can also practice walking meditation. Walk in silence. Commune with

the natural world. You will start to see and feel with a deeper awareness which arises from experiencing the world not from the intellect, but from a deeper level of your being. These times of inner silence allow you to find truth and nourishment for your everyday living. In silence, there is no purpose, no set agenda. There is nothing to plan and no outer activity to be accomplished. It is a time to simply be. It is an open space. Be who you are. And the great Being you are, will transform your life."

Ernest Holmes, the philosopher and mystic, expressed the magic of silence with the words: "I have listened to the great Silence; and in the deep places of Life, I have stood naked and receptive to Thy songs and they have entered my soul."[48]

Silence and meditation is the root of all mystical traditions which all centre around a belief in Oneness and our connection with it. A mystic can be defined as someone who intuitively senses Reality (the greater, or true, reality behind *maya*, or illusion). The mystic feels in union with the Infinite and beyond that, has a deep knowing that all life, visible and invisible, is the fullness and wholeness of God. A mystic is certainly not perfect all the time. However, as a mystic, you are mindful and aware of your thoughts, words, and actions. You lovingly embrace both the light and shadow of your being, shining the light of awareness on all of it and in this way integrating all parts of yourself. According to the unicorns, we are all evolving mystics. As you are open, receptive, and available to the innermost Presence, you realize and live your personal mysticism ever more fully.

The Universal Secret

In the ancient world, cosmic and religious mysteries were taught only to a select few, to the "privileged" initiates of secret religious orders. The "mysteries" that were taught were usually metaphysical or philosophical secrets. However, in the apostle's letter to the Colossians, Paul reveals that he became a minister in order to disclose "the mystery" in depth to as many people as possible. This "mystery" is a universal revelation, open to all of us. That means, open to *every human being*, including you. But what is the "secret", the "mystery"? According to Paul, it is "Christ in you, the hope and glory". What does this mean, and what is its purpose?

The Greek term "Christ" comes from the Aramaic-Hebrew word "Messiah". In Hebrew scriptures "Messiah" literally translates to "the anointed one". The spiritual and metaphysical meaning of "anointment" is someone who has been "anointed" with higher seeing; that is, someone who is "illumined" or "enlightened" – filled and enlightened with the power and presence of God. Jesus of Nazareth was an example of the perfect expression of the "Christ" in human form; for this reason he became known as Jesus the Christ, or Jesus Christ. The prophet and teacher from Galilee demonstrated the kingdom of heaven on earth through his powerful healing and teaching ministry. But his mission did not end there; his deeper intention was to reveal the power of the "Christ" consciousness and to awaken every human heart's potential and capacity to manifest the rich, spiritual dimensions of heaven on earth.

Following his example, we realize that the purpose of the Christ consciousness within us is not only for self-realization, but for the kingdom of heaven wherever we may be. Through the realization of the Christ consciousness, the God-Mind within, we become fulfilled and complete individuals -- awakened to our authentic self, our soul's purpose. The Indian mystic Swami Krishnananda puts it this way, "That higher awakening is called God-consciousness. In that condition, you will see that all the objects of the world are your own universal self".

The unicorns are here to lovingly guide you into this awakening to your true purpose. When you have "awakened", which simply means to wake up from the dream of illusion and remember who you really are, you are free to live life as it is intended to be – full of joy, creative expression and love. Ernest Holmes said, "When Christ dwells in us in love, which is unity, we are able to understand the things that the saints have understood. Saint simply means an unusually good and wise man – all saints have been human beings just as we are, for God makes all people alike. The universe plays no favourites."

How do you express the Christ within? The first and most important step is to let go of the small ego-mind, the conditioned and limited part of you that tells the story of "who you are" in this life; the part of you that carries all your resentments, your grief, and your unprocessed pain. The thirteenth century German mystic Meister Eckhart explained that, "God does not ask anything else except that you let yourself go and let God be God in you". When God is allowed to work through you, you discover that, in Meister Eckhart's words, "God's ground is my ground and my ground is God's ground. Here I live on my own. All our works should work out of this innermost ground without a why or a wherefore. Then, God and the soul do one work together eternally and very fruitfully. Then all that this person works, God works. And just as I can do almost nothing without God, so too God can accomplish nothing apart from me."

You are wanted and needed by all the universe, because you are a unique expression of the Mind of God. Nobody can be, do or express exactly what you can be, do, or express. The entire universe benefits when you let go of self-imposed limitations and free yourself to be the unique expression of God that you are. Swami Danavir, an Indian teacher and mystic, says "God Consciousness is what we are here for. It is the unfinished business we have left". When you experience yourself as the Divine emanation you are, you are free to express yourself authentically, free from the conditions and limitations of the intellect and the ego-story of this "one small life". You start to develop a *cosmic sense*, as the French philosopher and mystic Teilhard de Chardin called it: "The cosmos is fundamentally and primarily living. Christ [the God-Mind] is internal to the world, rooted in the world, even in the very heart of the tiniest atom. Nothing seems to me more vital, from the point of view of human energy, than the appearance and eventually, the systematic cultivation of such a cosmic sense."

Human beings live in two worlds – the world of matter, and the world of consciousness. Both of these natures come calling your attention, even within yourself. In the Bible these two natures are symbolized in Adam, the "man of earth" and Christ, the "man of God". One is our substance, and the other is our shadow. One is Real, and the other is Unreal, from an ultimate point of view. Intellect is the Adam intelligence, naming and labelling by material names, perceiving matter as real. The Christ nature is the Light of God within us. It is that part of us which is eternal. Understanding this you release all fear; you *know* you are free, loved and powerful. You understand the nature and purpose of your life. You understand God.

The inner mystical trinity whispers the eternal truths in your ear and the unicorns gallop across fields of gold in wild joy and abandon, their manes fluttering in the wind and their energy horns radiating spiritual light into the world.

"As God I realize that all is Good", says the Divine Oneness within you.
"As Mind I realize that all is Mind", says the Divine Mind.
"As Spirit I realize that all is Love", says the Holy Spirit within you.

Endnotes

1. Peter Kelder and Bernie Siegel, *Ancient Secret of the Fountain of Youth* (New York, NY: Doubleday, 1999)
2. Thomas Moore, *Dark Nights of the Soul* (London: Piatkus, 2004)
3. K.L. Seshagiri Rao, *Mahatma Gandhi and Comparative Religion* (Delhi: Motilal Banarsidass, 1990): p. 16
4. Jan Mirehiel, *Bell's Theorem To The Art Bell Effect*, available at <http://www.apocatastasis.net/God/PRIMARYFIELD/Bells-Theorem.html>
5. Larry Dossey, *Space, Time and Medicine* (Boston: Shambala Publishing, 1982): p. 100
6. David Bohm, Lee Nichol (ed), *The Essential David Bohm* (London: Routledge, 2003): p. 79
7. Sivananda (ed), *The Bhagavad Gita* (Rishikesh: Divine Life Society, 1969): p. 376
8. Foundation for Inner Peace, *A Course in Miracles: Combined Volume* (Mill Valley, CA: Foundation for Inner Peace, 1992): p. 14
9. Cat Saunders, "100% Responsibility and the Promise of a Hot Fudge Sundae: An Interview with Ihaleakala Hew Len", available at <http://www.drcat.org/articles_interviews/html/hotfudge.html>
10. Ibid.
11. Edgar Evans Cayce, Hugh Lynn Cayce (ed) *Edgar Cayce on Atlantis* (New York, NY: Grand Central Publishing, 1968): p. 104
12. Stephen Hawking, *Does God Play Dice?*, available at <http://www.hawking.org.uk/index.php/lectures/64>
13. Napoleon Hill, Think and Grow Rich: The Original Classic (Oxford: Capstone, 2009)
14. Matthew Fox, Meditations with Meister Eckhart (Rochester, VT: Bear & Company, 1983): p. 94

15. *Melinda Smith, Gina Kemp, and Jeanne Segal, Laughter is strong medicine for mind and body, available at* <http://www.helpguide.org/life/humor_laughter_health.htm>

16. Lao-Tzu, *Tao Te Ching* (Sioux Falls, SD: NuVision Publications): p. 44

17. Jalāl al-Dīn Rūmī (Maulana), Jelaluddin Rumi, Kabir Edmund Helminski, *Love is a Stranger: Selected Lyric Poetry of Jelaluddin Rumi* (Boston: Shambhala Publications, 2000): p. 49

18. Joseph Murphy, *The Power of Your Subconscious Mind* (Upper Saddle River, NJ: Prentice Hall Press, 2008): p. 129

19. Leonard Willoughby, *Every Day Tao: Self-Help in the Here and Now* (San Francisco, CA: Red Wheel/Weiser, 2001): p. 39.

20. Alice Anne Parker, *Understand Your Dreams* (Novato, CA: H J Kramer, 2001)

21. *Number and the Cosmos*, 1-3, available at <Astronomy.pomona.edu/archeo/greece/pythagoras/ideas.htm>

22. Ralph Waldo Emerson, *Essays* (London: John Chapman, 1853): p. 138

23. Eknath Easwaran, *The Upanishads* (Petaluma, CA: Nilgiri Press, 1987): p. 37

24. Donald Gowan, *Theology in Exodus: Biblical Theology in the Form of a Commentary* (Louisville, KY: John Knox Press, 1994): p. 84

25. Deepak Chopra, *Creating Health: How to Wake Up the Body's Intelligence* (New York, NY: Houghton Mifflin, 1987): p. 157

26. Isabelle Stengers, *Power and Invention: Situating Science* (Minneapolis, MN: University of Minnesota Press, 1997): p. 45

27. Hari Prasad Shastri, *The World Within the Mind (Yoga-Vasishtha): Extracts from the Discourses of the Sage Vasishtha to His Pupil, Prince Rama, and the Story of Queen Chudala* (London: Shanti Sadan,1975): p.20

28. Glen Rein, Mike Atkinson, and Rollin McCraty, "The Physiological and Psychological Effects of Compassion and Anger", *Journal of Advancement in Medicine*, vol. 8, no. 2 (1995): pp. 87-105

29. For more information, visit http://www.glcoherence. org/monitoring-system/about-system.html.

30. Sriramakrishna Matha, *The Vedanta Kesari* (Mylapore, Madras: Sri Ramakrishna Matha, 1996): p. 477

31. Victor Gollancz, *From Darkness to Light: A Confession of Faith in the Form of an Anthology* (New York, NY: Harper,1956): p. 529

32. Gaurev Pradhan, *Rabrindranath Tagore: Literary Concepts* (New Delhi: A. P. H. Publishing Corporation, 2002): p. 96

33. Charles Fillmore, *Christian Healing: The Science of Being* (Whitefish, MT: Kessinger Publishing Co., 2005): p. 5

34. Russell Goodman, *Pragmatism: Critical Concepts in Philosophy* (Abingdon, Oxfordshire: Routledge, 2005): p.196

35. Swami Vivekananda, *Jnana Yoga: The Yoga of Knowledge* (Kolkata: Trio Process, 2007 [1915]): p. 132-133

36. William Shakespeare, *Hamlet* (London: Nick Hern, 2001 [c.1599-1601]): p. 263

37. Ralph Waldo Emerson, *The Essential Writings of Ralph Waldo Emerson* (New York, NY: Modern Library, 2000 [1841]): p. 132

38. Henry Reed, *Awakening Your Psychic Powers* (New York, NY: St. Martin's Press, 1988): p. 19

39. Charles Tart, *Transpersonal Psychologies* (London: Routledge, 1975): p. 156

40. Kevin J. Todeschi, *Edgar Cayce on the Akashic Records* (Virginia Beach, VA: A.R.E Press, 1998): p. xvi

41. Taizan Maezumi, *On Zen Practice: Body, Breath, Mind* (Boston: Wisdom Publications, 2002): p. 20

42. Paul Tillich, *The Shaking of the Foundations: Sermons* (Middlesex: Penguin, 1962): p. 46

43. Ernest Holmes, *The Science of Mind* (New York, NY: R.M. McBride and Co, 1938): p. 388

44. Ernest Holmes, Jesse Jennings, *The Essential Ernest Holmes* (New York, NY: J.P. Tarcher/ Putnam, 2002): p. 222

45. Ernest Holmes, *The Science of Mind*: p. 127-128

46. Ernest Holmes, The Science of Mind: p. 377

47. Edwin Arnold (trans), *The Song Celestial: Or, Bhagavadgita (from the Mahabharata): Being a Discourse between Arjuna, Prince of India, and the Supreme Being under the form of Krishna* (London: Routledge & Kegan Paul, 1952): p. 9

48. Ernest Holmes, *The Science of Mind*: p. 367

Bibliography

Edwin Arnold (trans), *The Song Celestial: Or, Bhagavad-gita (from the Mahabharata): Being a Discourse between Arjuna, Prince of India, and the Supreme Being under the form of Krishna* (London: Routledge & Kegan Paul, 1952)

David Bohm, Lee Nichol (ed), *The Essential David Bohm* (London: Routledge, 2003)

Edgar Evans Cayce, Hugh Lynn Cayce (ed) *Edgar Cayce on Atlantis* (New York, NY: Grand Central Publishing, 1968)

Deepak Chopra, *Creating Health: How to Wake Up the Body's Intelligence* (New York, NY: Houghton Mifflin, 1987)

Larry Dossey, *Space, Time and Medicine* (Boston: Shambala Publishing, 1982)

Eknath Easwaran, *The Upanishads* (Petaluma, CA: Nilgiri Press, 1987)

Ralph Waldo Emerson, *Essays* (London: John Chapman, 1853)

Ralph Waldo Emerson, *The Essential Writings of Ralph Waldo Emerson* (New York, NY: Modern Library, 2000 [1841])

Charles Fillmore, *Christian Healing: The Science of Being* (Whitefish, MT: Kessinger, 2005)

Foundation for Inner Peace, *A Course in Miracles: Combined Volume* (Mill Valley, CA: Foundation for Inner Peace, 1992)

Matthew Fox, *Meditations with Meister Eckhart* (Rochester, VT: Bear & Company, 1983)

Victor Gollancz, *From Darkness to Light: A Confession of Faith in the Form of an Anthology* (New York, NY: Harper,1956)

Russell Goodman, *Pragmatism: Critical Concepts in Philosophy* (Abingdon, Oxfordshire: Routledge, 2005)

Donald Gowan, *Theology in Exodus: Biblical Theology in the Form of a Commentary* (Louisville, KY: John Knox Press, 1994)

Napoleon Hill, *Think and Grow Rich: The Original Classic* (Oxford: Capstone, 2009)

Ernest Holmes, Jesse Jennings (ed), *The Essential Ernest Holmes* (New York, NY: J.P. Tarcher/ Putnam, 2002)

Ernest Holmes, *The Science of Mind* (New York, NY: R.M. McBride and Co, 1938)

Peter Kelder and Bernie Siegel, *Ancient Secret of the Fountain of Youth* (New York, NY: Doubleday, 1999)

Lao-Tzu, *Tao Te Ching* (Sioux Falls, SD: NuVision Publications)

Taizan Maezumi, *On Zen Practice: Body, Breath, Mind* (Boston: Wisdom Publications, 2002)

Thomas Moore, *Dark Nights of the Soul* (London: Piatkus, 2004)

Joseph Murphy, *The Power of Your Subconscious Mind* (Upper Saddle River, NJ: Prentice Hall Press, 2008)

Alice Anne Parker, *Understand Your Dreams* (Novato, CA: H J Kramer, 2001)

Gaurev Pradhan, *Rabrindranath Tagore: Literary Concepts* (New Delhi: A. P. H. Publishing Corporation, 2002)

Henry Reed, *Awakening Your Psychic Powers* (New York, NY: St. Martin's Press, 1988)

Glen Rein, Mike Atkinson, and Rollin McCraty, "The Physiological and Psychological Effects of Compassion and Anger", *Journal of Advancement in Medicine*, vol. 8, no. 2 (1995)

Jalāl al-Dīn Rūmī (Maulana), Jelaluddin Rumi, Kabir Edmund Helminski, *Love is a Stranger: Selected Lyric Poetry of Jelaluddin Rumi* (Boston, MA: Shambhala Publications, 2000)

K.L. Seshagiri Rao, *Mahatma Gandhi and Comparative Religion* (Delhi: Motilal Banarsidass, 1990)

William Shakespeare, *Hamlet* (London: Nick Hern, 2001 [c.1599-1601])

Hari Prasad Shastri, *The World Within the Mind (Yoga-Vasishtha): Extracts from the Discourses of the Sage Vasishtha to His Pupil, Prince Rama, and the Story of Queen Chudala* (London: Shanti Sadan,1975)

Sivananda (ed), *The Bhagavad Gita* (Rishikesh: Divine Life Society, 1969)

Sriramakrishna Matha, *The Vedanta Kesari* (Mylapore, Madras: Sri Ramakrishna Matha, 1996)

Isabelle Stengers, *Power and Invention: Situating Science* (Minneapolis, MN: University of Minnesota Press, 1997)

Charles Tart, *Transpersonal Psychologies* (London: Routledge, 1975)

Paul Tillich, *The Shaking of the Foundations: Sermons* (Middlesex, UK: Penguin Books, 1962)

Kevin J. Todeschi, *Edgar Cayce on the Akashic Records* (Virginia Beach, VA: A.R.E Press, 1998)

Swami Vivekananda, *Jnana Yoga: The Yoga of Knowledge* (Kolkata: Trio Process, 2007 [1915])

Leonard Willoughby, *Every Day Tao: Self-Help in the Here and Now* (San Francisco, CA: Red Wheel/Weiser, 2001)